California Natural History Guides: 32

SIERRA WILDFLOWERS

Mt. Lassen to Kern Canyon

BY

THEODORE F. NIEHAUS

UNIVERSITY OF CALIFORNIA PRESS

BERKELEY • LOS ANGELES • LONDON

ACKNOWLEDGMENTS

Permission to use appropriate illustrations from Willis Linn Jepson's *A Manual of the Flowering Plants of California*, and *Flora of California* was granted by the Trustees of the Jepson Herbarium, University of California. The plant part illustrations were drawn by Mary Ann Schwartz and the map of the Sierra Nevada region by Barbara Thatcher. All color photographs are by the author. I am appreciative of the assistance received from my colleagues, and the hundreds of helpful suggestions from my numerous trail companions and the hikers who stopped to watch as the field research was in progress and offered additional observations for consideration.

CONTENTS

General Abbreviations 4

Introduction 5

Identification of Wildflowers.................... 9

    Equipment Needed 10

    Preparation 10

    Wildflower Habitats 11

    Flowering Times 11

Master Key To Common Sierra Nevada
    Wildflowers 11

Useful References 207

Index to Families, Genera, and Species.........209

Cover Photographs
Upper left: *Castilleja lemmonii*—Lemmons Paint Brush.
Upper right: *Calochortus leichtlinii*—Leichtlin's Mariposa Tulip.
Lower left: *Wyethia mollis*—Mountain Mule Ears.
Lower right: *Sarcodes sanguinea*—Snow Plant.

GENERAL ABBREVIATIONS

cm—centimeter
Co.—County
dm—decimeter
e.—east
e. slope—east slope of Sierra Nevada
fl, fls—flower, flowers
lf, lvs—leaf, leaves
m—meters
mm—millimeters
subsp—subspecies
var.—variety
w.—west
w. slope—west slope of Sierra Nevada

INTRODUCTION

The nearly 550 wildflowers described in this guide represent the common ones, both native and introduced, found in the different plant communities or zones of the Sierra Nevada. I have also included a few less common species that are especially interesting. I drove and hiked throughout the Sierra Nevada many times to be sure this book would contain the wildflowers most likely to be seen about resort areas, National Parks, country roads, and remote regions reached only by backpacking.

Wildflowers, by definition, are those plants which normally develop all, or nearly all, of their above-ground parts in one growing season and die back at the end of the year. The trees and shrubs of the Sierra Nevada are described in separate books in this series.

The area covered in this guide extends from the mountain region of Mt. Lassen National Park south to Kern Canyon along Highway 178 in Kern County; the western boundary begins at the Foothill Woodland Forest just above the Central Valley Grassland; and the eastern boundary runs along Highway 395. A small region on the southeast corner (Joshua Tree Woodland) near Walker Pass is not included.

Properly identifying a wildflower that you suddenly discover while you are hiking can be a tremendously satisfying experience. Knowing the color and shape of the flower is not enough—you should become familiar with the characteristics of the leaves, stems, sepals, and other plant parts. Knowledge of the plant's habitat—the kind of place where a particular species grows—is helpful, too. Some species require a specific zone or altitude; some grow only in dry, well-drained places while

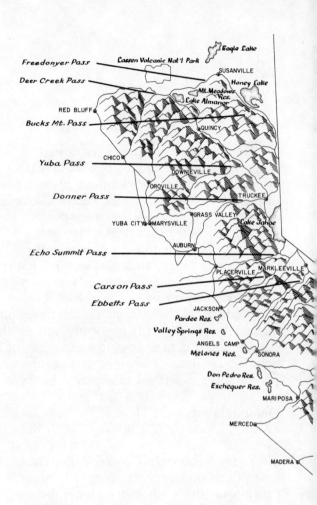

Freedonyer Pass
Lassen Volcanic Nat'l Park
Eagle Lake
SUSANVILLE
Deer Creek Pass
Honey Lake
Mt. Meadows
Res.
Lake Almanor
RED BLUFF
Bucks Mt. Pass
QUINCY
Yuba Pass
CHICO
DOWNIEVILLE
OROVILLE
TRUCKEE
Donner Pass
GRASS VALLEY
Lake Tahoe
YUBA CITY MARYSVILLE
AUBURN
Echo Summit Pass
MARKLEEVILLE
PLACERVILLE
Carson Pass
Ebbetts Pass
JACKSON
Pardee Res.
Valley Springs Res.
ANGELS CAMP
Melones Res. SONORA
Don Pedro Res.
Exchequer Res.
MARIPOSA
MERCED
MADERA

MAP OF THE SIERRA NEVADA

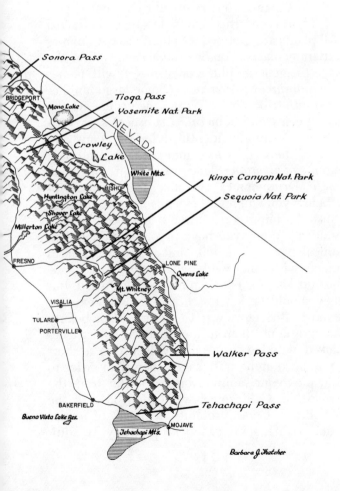

Sonora Pass

BRIDGEPORT

Mono Lake

Tioga Pass

Yosemite Nat. Park

NEVADA

Crowley Lake

White Mts.

BISHOP

Kings Canyon Nat. Park

Sequoia Nat. Park

Huntington Lake

Shaver Lake

Millerton Lake

FRESNO

LONE PINE

Owens Lake

Mt. Whitney

VISALIA

TULARE

PORTERVILLE

Walker Pass

BAKERFIELD

Tehachapi Pass

Bueno Vista Lake Res.

MOJAVE

Tehachapi Mts.

Barbara J. Thatcher

others are found in moist, swampy spots; some prefer full sun, some like shade, or some want a little of both. In the descriptions of the individual species in this guide you will find such information, as well as facts about how the plants reproduce, the months when they may be in flower, whether insects or birds are the pollinators, how man has made use of the plant, why the plant name was chosen or who discovered the species, and sometimes folklore about the plant.

Because common names for wildflowers can be misleading and often do not distinguish among the many species within a genus, you are urged to become accustomed to identifying the plants by their botanical names. All plants are grouped into families, with names such as Ranunculaceae or Saxifragaceae. Within the families are the genera (plural of "genus"), with names such as *Delphinium* or *Anemone*. (Some large families are divided into tribes first.) Within the genera are the individual species and sometimes subspecies or varieties. A plant is usually identified by its genus and species name, followed by its common name—examples, *Delphinium gracilentum*, Slender Larkspur; *Anemone drummondii*, Drummond's Anemone. (In the descriptive lists below you will find the genus name is abbreviated to just the initial letter after it has been spelled out fully once.) When you have become familiar with the botanical names, you will find it much easier to communicate with other wildflower enthusiasts.

Wildflowers should not be picked or disturbed, but rather they should be left for the next observer to enjoy. The most satisfactory way to preserve their beauty is by photographing them in their natural habitat, because picked wildflowers usually wilt within a short time. If you absolutely must have a flower in order to identify it, pick your sample from a spot far from the trail or roadside. California law, Section 384a of the California Penal Code prohibits removal of entire plants from private, state, or federal property. In addi-

[8]

tion some endangered species are specifically protected. The National Park and Forest Services have their own regulations as well.

The seeds and bulbs of wildflowers are usually dormant during the summer, and they will not germinate or grow when it is warm. Landowners in the Sierra Nevada can help preserve wildflowers by not watering the wildflower habitats during the summer months; such watering promotes the growth of fungi which attack and destroy the seeds. Plowing is also disastrous to wildflowers.

Organizations devoted to protecting wildflowers are listed in the reference section at the end of this book. Other groups from which you can learn more about wildflowers and where you can share your experiences are listed, too.

Although many of the plants described in this guide were considered edible by the native California Indians, and although information about how they were used is given, it is unwise to prepare any plant for food without knowing how to process it to remove any possible poisonous properties. There are books about the use of wild plants as food which give details concerning preparation.

This guide was planned for use in the field.

IDENTIFICATION OF WILDFLOWERS

To find the name of a particular Sierra Nevada flower you have discovered, you can compare it with the pictures in this book—but that is a slow and often frustrating method. The best and scientific way is to use the keys given in this guide. The Master Key will lead you to the family name. From there you go to the key or section on that particular family, and then to the genus key or section, and finally to the species and common name, where the flower will be described in detail. It's a little like a treasure hunt, and you will need some equipment and preparation.

(1) A small hand lens 10× or 15× for examining flower parts. (2) A thin insect pin to serve as a tiny knife to open flower parts. (3) A metric ruler (all scientific measurements are in the metric system). On the inside front cover and near each of the large family keys you will find a metric ruler printed.

PREPARATION

1. Learn the plant part names and shapes used throughout this book by studying the Master Key (p. 11) and the accompanying illustrations (figs. 1–8).

2. Look at the wildflower you want to identify and study its parts and their shapes.

3. Learn to use the keys. A key consists of numbered pairs of contrasting statements. Only one statement of each pair will apply to the wildflower you are trying to identify; the other will not. Each statement concludes either with "see" followed by a number or with a botanical name—this is the clue that leads you on to the next step in the treasure hunt. (In this guide keys have been omitted for the smaller families and genera.)

Step 1. In the Master Key below, decide which statement in the first pair applies to your wildflower. Move on to the numbered pair it tells you to "see."

Step 2. Continue this process until you arrive at a statement that ends with a botanical family name. Turn to the page listed.

Step 3. In the family key, follow the same procedure until you arrive at a statement that ends in a genus name.

Step 4. Go to that genus key, or if there is none, go directly to the genus and species descriptions which will follow.

Step 5. Find the species description that fits your wildflower. If no description fits, you may have made the wrong choice in one of the earlier steps, so go back to a pair of statements in the keys where you may have been uncertain and try the alternate statement.

Step 6. If you still fail to find the correct description, compare your wildflower with the pictures and try to determine which plant family it resembles most. Then use that family key.

Soon you will recognize that some wildflowers are

very similar to others. These similarities determine the botanical classifications. Closely related species are classified in the same genus. Closely related genera are classified in one family. After just a little study you should be able to recognize the common families or genera on sight. Then you can go directly to the family or genus key.

The descriptions include brief remarks about the habitats of each species. If you keep in mind the kind of place where you see a wildflower growing, when you come to a similar habitat you may recognize the species immediately. The range of elevation above sea level where each species occurs is given (in feet) in this guide, too.

The larger biotic communities in which a species grows are abbreviated in the descriptions as follows (for a complete discussion see *Natural History of The Sierra Nevada* by Arthur C. Smith):

A—Alpine
C—Chaparral
FG—Foothill Grassland
FM—Freshwater Marsh
FW—Foothill Woodland
MCF—Mixed Coniferous Forest

MM—Mountain Meadow
PJ—Pinon-Juniper Woodland
YPF—Ponderosa Pine Forest
S—Subalpine Forest
SS—Sagebrush-Shadscale Shrub
SL—Lakes and Ponds

FLOWERING TIMES

The months when the species might be in flower are at the end of each description, but remember these represent a broad range. The earliest month shown is for the lowest elevation limit of that particular species and the latest month is for the upper elevation limit.

MASTER KEY TO
COMMON SIERRA NEVADA WILDFLOWERS

1a—Petals lacking or only sepals present. See 2.
1b—Petals present and evident. See 5.

2a—Fls without any sepals or petals, sap milky. *Euphorbiaceae*, p. 36.

2b—Fls with sepals, not petals (*Polygonaceae* may appear as if having colored petals. Follow this lead for *Polygonaceae*.) See 3.

3a—Fls (actually sepals) dark brownish-red. *Asarum*, p. 155.

3b—Fls not as in 3a. See 4.

4a—Stamens 3–9. *Polygonaceae*, p. 70.

4b—Stamens 10 or many. *Thalictrum*, p. 27.

5a—Sepals and petals of each fl in 4's or 5's or multiples. Class Dicotyledonae. See 6.

5b—Sepals and petals of each fl in 3's or multiples. See Class Monocotyledonae, p. 191.

6a—Petals free from each other, or almost so. See 7.

6b—Petals fused together. See 32.

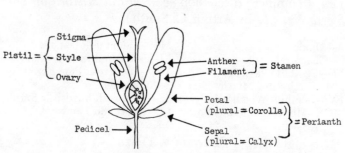

SUPERIOR OVARY POSITION

This term refers to a flower with sepals, petals, and stamens attached *below* the ovary.

Fig. 1

7a—Stamens numerous, *more than* twice as many as petals. See 8.

7b—Stamens *not* more than twice as many as petals. See 23.

8a—Ovary superior. See 9.

8b—Ovary partially or completely inferior. See 17.

9a—Pond plants, large floating lvs. *Nuphar*, p. 28.
9b—Mostly land plants, without floating lvs. See 10.

10a—Sepals 2. See 11.
10b—Sepals more than 2. See 12.

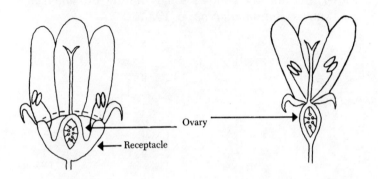

Ovary

Receptacle

PARTIAL OVARY
POSITION

This term refers to a flower with sepals, petals, and stamens attached *part way* up the side of the cup-shaped receptacle around the ovary.

INFERIOR OVARY
POSITION

This term refers to a flower with sepals, petals, and stamens attached on *top* of the ovary.

Fig. 2

11a—Sepals remaining after fl opens, plants fleshy. *Portulacaceae*, p. 65.
11b—Sepals falling off when fl opens, sap milky. *Papaveraceae*, p. 40.

12a—Stamens fused into tube. *Malvaceae*, p. 28.
12b—Stamens free from each other. See 13.

13a—Insectivorous plants, lf a tall tubelike pitcher. *Sarraceniaceae*, p. 29.
13b—Not as in 13a. See 14.

14a—Lvs very thick, plants succulent. *Crassulaceae*, p. 128.
14b—Lvs thin. See 15.

15a—Lvs. opposite. *Hypericaceae*, p. 39.
15b—Lvs alternate. See 16.

16a—Petals maroon; sepals remaining when fl opens. *Paeoniaceae*, p. 27.
16b—Petals mostly yellow; sepals falling off when fl opens. *Ranunculaceae*, p. 19.

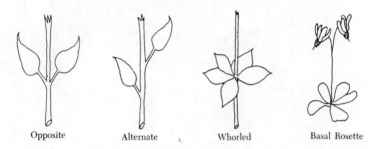

Opposite   Alternate   Whorled   Basal Rosette

LEAF ARRANGEMENTS ON STEM

Fig. 3

17a—Ovary partially inferior (stamens attached half-way down fl tube on ovary). See 18.
17b—Ovary completely inferior. See 19.

18a—Stipules present below lf petiole. *Rosaceae*, p. 134.
18b—Stipules absent. *Saxifragaceae*, p. 130.

19a—Vines with small spiny melonlike fruit. *Cucurbitaceae*, p. 164.

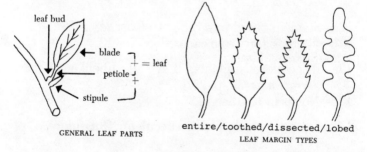

leaf bud

blade ⎤
        ⎬ + = leaf
petiole ⎦ +

stipule

GENERAL LEAF PARTS

entire/toothed/dissected/lobed
LEAF MARGIN TYPES

Fig. 4

[14]

19b—Not vines. See 20.

20a—Petals 4. *Onagraceae*, p. 151.
20b—Petals 5. See 21.

21a—Fls in umbels. See 22.
21b—Fls not in umbels, fls in a raceme. *Loasaceae*, p. 36.

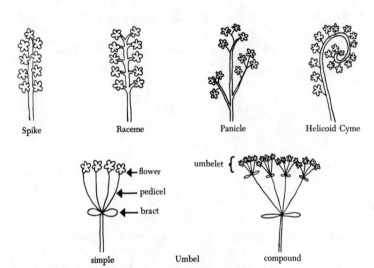

Spike   Raceme   Panicle   Helicoid Cyme

umbelet {

← flower
← pedicel
← bract

simple   Umbel   compound

Spike: The individual flowers are without pedicels and are on a single non-branching stem.
Raceme: The individual flowers are with a pedicel and are on a single non-branching stem.
Panicle: The flowers have a pedicel and are on a branched stem.
Helicoid Cyme: A coiled branching stem with the youngest flowers at the tip.
Umbel: All the flowers have pedicels and are attached at the same point.

Fig. 5

22a—Styles 4–6. *Araliaceae*, p. 155.
22b—Styles 2. *Umbelliferae*, p. 156.

23a—Styles 2–5, divided nearly to base. See 24.
23b—Style 1, not divided or only slightly. See 27.

24a—Upper lf surface with conspicuous red glandular hairs, bog plants. *Droseraceae*, p. 29.
24b—Upper lf surface without red hairs. See 25.

25a—Sepals 2. *Portulacaceae*, p. 65.
25b—Sepals 3 or more. See 26.

26a—Lvs opposite. *Caryophyllaceae*, p. 58.
26b—Lvs alternate. *Linaceae*, p. 35.

27a—Petals 4. *Cruciferae*, p. 43.
27b—Petals 5. See 28.

28a—All petals of same size and shape in 1 flower (= fl regular shape). See 29.
28b—Two or more petal shapes and sizes in 1 flower (= fl irregular). See 31.

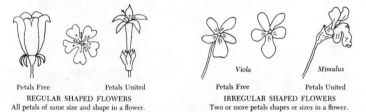

Petals Free Petals United
REGULAR SHAPED FLOWERS
All petals of same size and shape in a flower.

Viola *Mimulus*
Petals Free Petals United
IRREGULAR SHAPED FLOWERS
Two or more petals shapes or sizes in a flower.

Fig. 6

29a—Ovary a capsule with many seeds. *Pyrolaceae*, p. 81.
29b—Ovary separating into 1-seeded units. See 30.

30a—Lower lvs opposite, seeds long tailed. *Geraniaceae*, p. 31.
30b—Lower lvs alternate, seeds rounded nutlets. *Limnanthaceae*, p. 34.

31a—Fls pealike (see fig. 136 on p. 141). *Leguminosae*, p. 139.
31b—Fls violetlike (see fig. 6). *Violaceae*, p. 37.

32a—Ovary superior. See 33.
32b—Ovary inferior. See 46.

33a—Plant stem white, brown, or red. *Pyrolaceae*, p. 81.
33b—Plant stem green. See 34.

34a—All petals of same size and shape in one flower (= fl regular shape). See 35.

34b—Two or more petal shapes and sizes in one flower (= fl irregular). See 44.

35a—Plants with milky sap. See 36.
35b—Plants without milky sap. See 37.

36a—Fls in large umbels. *Asclepiadaceae*, p. 88.
36b—Fls single or in racemes. *Apocynaceae*, p. 87.

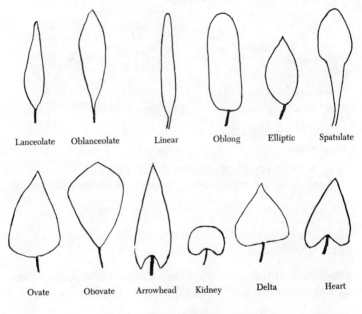

Lanceolate Oblanceolate Linear Oblong Elliptic Spatulate

Ovate Obovate Arrowhead Kidney Delta Heart

LEAF SHAPES

Fig. 7

37a—Stamens as many as the petals and *opposite* them. *Primulaceae*, p. 77.

37b—Stamens as many as the petals and *alternate* with them. See 38.

38a—Tiny brownish fls, many at the top of a leafless

[17]

stalk. *Plantaginaceae*, p. 80.
38b—Fls not brownish. See 39.

39a—Ovary of 4 nutlets (look where oldest fl *was*).
   Boraginaceae, p. 104.
39b—Ovary a single capsule. See 40.

40a—Style tip 3-cleft. *Polemoniaceae*, p. 90.
40b—Style tip 1- or 2-lobed or cleft. See 41.

41a—Style tip 1, entire. See 42.
41b—Style tip 2-lobed. See 43.

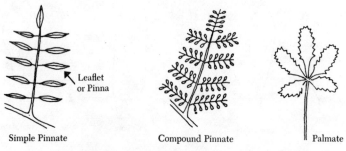

Simple Pinnate   Compound Pinnate   Palmate

TYPES OF COMPOUND LEAVES
Each of the above represents one complete compound leaf.

Fig. 8

42a—Lvs opposite. *Gentianaceae*, p. 84.
42b—Lvs alternate. *Solanaceae*, p. 107.

43a—Stem trailing or vinelike. *Convolvulaceae*, p. 89.
43b—Stem erect, fls in a coiled cyme. *Hydrophyllaceae*,
   p. 98.

44a—Fl distinctly flattened. *Fumariaceae*, p. 42.
44b—Fl tubular at least near base. See 45.

45a—Fruit of 4 nutlets, stem 4-sided. *Labiatae*, p. 125.
45b—Fruit a single capsule, stems rounded. *Scrophulariaceae*, p. 108.

46a—Stamens separate. See 47.
46b—Stamens fused into a tube. See 49.

[18]

47a—Lvs alternately arranged. *Campanulaceae*, p. 165.
47b—Lvs opposite or whorled. See 48.

48a—Lvs opposite. *Valerianaceae*, p. 163.
48b—Lvs in whorls, stem squarish. *Rubiaceae*, p. 163.

49a—Vine with tendrils, and spiny melonlike fruit. *Cucurbitaceae*, p. 164.
49b—Stem usually erect, never vinelike, many small fls in a single sunflowerlike head. *Compositae*, p. 166.

KEY TO THE FAMILY
RANUNCULACEAE (CROWFOOT)

1a—Fruit capsulelike or berries. See 2.
1b—Fruit a cluster of separate, 1-seeded achenes. See 6.

2a—Fl irregular, i.e., 2 or more petal shapes and sizes in 1 flower. See 3.
2b—Fl regular, i.e., all petals of same size and shape in 1 flower. See 4.

3a—Upper sepal a long colored spur. *Delphinium*.
3b—Upper sepal a colored hood. *Aconitum*.

4a—Petal bases long spurred. *Aquilegia*.
4b—Petal base not spurred. See 5.

5a—Lvs undivided. *Caltha*.
5b—Lvs compound. *Actaea*.

6a—Stem lvs whorled. *Anemone*.
6b—Stem lvs alternate or none. See 7.

7a—Petals present. *Ranunculus*.
7b—Petals absent, lvs compound. *Thalictrum*.

Key to the Genus *Delphinium* (Larkspur)

1a—Fl orange to dull red. *Delphinium nudicaule*.
1b—Fls blue to purple. See 2.

2a—Stem base slender, easily breaking. See 3.
2b—Stem base stout, difficult to break. See 6.

3a—Stem and lvs hairy. *D. pratense.*
3b—Stem and lvs mostly hairless. See 4.

4a—Outer side of sepals hairless. See 5.
4b—Outer side of sepals hairy. *D. nuttallianum.*

5a—Sepals 11–15 mm long, 6–15 fls. *D. patens.*
5b—Sepals 5–10 mm long, 15–20 fls. *D. gracilentum.*

6a—Plant 1–2 m tall. *D. glaucum.*
6b—Plant usually much less than 1 m tall. See 7.

7a—Fls pale blue to whitish. *D. hansenii.*
7b—Fls deep blue to purple. See 8.

8a—Lvs hairless, pentagonal shape. *D. polycladon.*
8b—Lvs hairy, with 5 narrow lobes. *D. andersonii.*

Cattle and horses can contract the usually fatal disease of delphinosis from eating delphiniums, which are the deadliest of all native California plants.

Delphinium nudicaule — Red Larkspur. Fls reddish-orange. Dry slopes in partial shade of trees, occasional below 7000 on w. slope. Yosemite north. FW, C. March–June.

D. pratense—Meadow Larkspur. Stem slender, 2.5–3 dm tall; lvs few, 6–10 fls. Meadows and open woods 6000–8500, southern Sierra. MM, MCF. June–July.

D. nuttallianum—Nuttall's Larkspur. Stem slender; lvs rounded, basal. Open areas 5000–10000. MCF, MM, C. May–July.

Named for Thomas Nuttall, who searched intensively for new plants throughout the United States in the early 1800s and visited California in 1835.

D. patens subsp. *greenei*—Spreading Larkspur. Lvs few, 3–parted, near stem base. Borders of woods below 3500 on w. slope. FW, C. March–May.

D. gracilentum—Slender Larkspur. Stem 2–4 dm long; lvs equally 5–parted, 4–5 cm wide. Damp places in partial shade below 8000 on w. slope. FW, MCF. April–July.

D. glaucum—Glaucous Larkspur. Stem stout, woody, 1–2 m tall; lvs 8–20 cm broad. Wet meadows or near streams, 5000–11000, Tioga Pass and north. MM, MCF. July–Sept.

D. hanseni—Hansen's Larkspur. Stem unbranched, 4–8 dm tall; lvs 5–parted, 2–5 cm wide with recurved hairs; sepals dark blue to nearly white; Fls with upper petals white. Dry grassy slopes among shrubs, 1000–3500 on w. slope. FG, FW, C. May–June.

D. polycladon — Many-branched Larkspur. Stems several, 5–8 dm tall; lvs round to reniform 3–10 cm wide, mostly 3–lobed; few-flowered raceme. In wet meadows and stream bottom amid lush growth. 7500–12000, along main crest. MM, MCF. July–Sept.

D. andersonii—Anderson's Larkspur. Stems without hairs, 2–6 dm tall, hollow; lvs rounded, 1–3 cm wide, at base of stem only, strongly divided. Dry sandy soils among shrubs and pines on e. slope from Lee Vining north, 5000–7600. MCF, C. May–July.

Genus *Aconitum*

Aconitum columbianum—Columbia Monkshood. Pl. 1a. Plant usually 5–20 dm tall; lvs broad, 3–5 cleft; fls purple, scattered along raceme, uppermost colored sepal similar to a monk's hood over rest of fl. Moist or wet places in meadows or willow thickets, widespread 4000–10000. MCF, MM. July–Aug.

All parts of plant are poisonous.

Genus *Actaea*

Actaea rubra subsp. *arguta* — Red Baneberry. Fig. 9. Stems stout, 4–8 dm tall; lvs pinnately compound. Damp woods and willow thickets, below 10000, widespread. MCF, MM. May–June.

The red berries are poisonous to man, but food for grouse and mice.

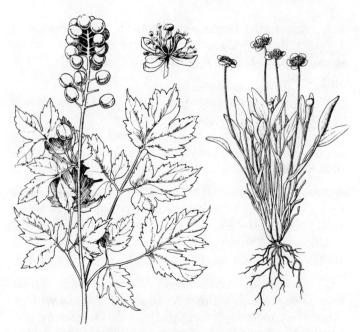

Fig. 9 *Actaea rubra*   Fig. 10 *Ranunculus alismaefolius*

Key to the Genus *Anemone* (Wind Flowers)

1a—Styles hairy, feathery in fruit. *A. occidentalis.*
1b—Styles hairless. *A. drummondii.*

Indians used the leaves of anemones to make a poultice for rheumatism. The two species flower immediately after the snow melts.

Anemone occidentalis — Pasque Flower. Fls white or purplish on short stem, which later elongates to 1–6 dm tall with a large round fruiting head with many long feathery styles. Frequently seen on open rocky slopes, 6000–11000, main crest. S, A. July–Aug.

A. drummondii—Drummond's Anemone. Pl. 1*b*. Fls white with blue tinted backs, on short stem. Open sandy slopes, 5000–12000, Mono, Sonora, and Donner passes. S, A. May–Aug.

Named for Thomas Drummond, an early botanical collector in the southwest.

[22]

Key to the Genus *Aquilegia* (Columbine)

1a—Fls scarlet, tinged with yellow. *A. formosa.*
1b—Fls cream with tints of purple. *A. pubescens.*

Besides the two true columbine species, intermediate hybrids resulting from cross-pollination by bumblebees can be found on talus slopes, an intermediate drainage between the poorly drained flats where *A. formosa* grows and the cliffs where *A. pubescens* grows. Many different colored hybrids can be seen near Saddlebag Lake, near Tioga Pass (Mono Co.), Rock Creek (Inyo Co.), Humphreys Basin (Fresno Co.) and elsewhere.

Aquilegia formosa — Crimson Columbine. Pl. 1c. Stem 5–10 dm tall; lvs 3-parted; fls crimson-orange, hanging downward. Common along stream banks, 4000–10000. MCF, S, MM. June–Aug.

The position of the flowers accommodates hummingbirds; they sip nectar and pollinate this species.

A. pubescens—Coville's Columbine. Pl. 1e. Lvs compound on stems 2–3 dm tall; fls cream with tints of purple. Rocky cliffs in alpine zone, 9000–13000. S, A. June–Aug.

It is believed that the cream-colored flower attracts a certain moth species seeking the nectar in the long flower spurs, which are the same length as the moth's proboscis; smaller moth species are effectively kept from using the same nectar source. In the process of obtaining nectar the moth pollinates the flower or carries the pollen to the next flower.

Genus *Caltha*

Caltha howellii — Marsh Marigold. Pl. 1d. Plant low, with fleshy kidney-shaped lvs and 1 white fl per stem. Common marshy places shortly after snow melts, 4000–11000. MCF, MM, S. May–July.

Key to the Genus *Ranunculus* (Buttercup)

1a—Fls white. *R. aquatilis.*
1b—Fls yellow (or creamy in 8a). See 2.

2a—Lvs lanceolate. *R. alismaefolius.*
2b—Lvs not as above. See 3.

3a—Lower lvs 3–7-parted. See 4.
3b—Lower lvs shallowly lobed. See 8.

4a—Seeds with a straight beak. See 5.
4b—Seeds with a hooked beak. See 6.

5a—Stems hairy. *R. orthorhynchus.*
5b—Stems not hairy. *R. eschscholtzii.*

6a—Plant tall, wiry stem. See 7.
6b—Plant low, stem and lvs fleshy. See 8.

7a—Fls with 5–6 petals. *R. occidentalis.*
7b—Fls with 7–16 petals. *R. californicus.*

8a—Fls creamy. *R. hystriculus.*
8b—Fls yellow. See 9.

9a—Seeds smooth. *R. flammula.*
9b—Seeds hairy and spiny. *R. muricatus.*

Indians parched the seeds of ranunculus to make flour meal for bread, and they boiled the leaves and stems and ate them, too. Birds and small mammals eat some parts of this species. However, the ranunculus is poisonous to humans in the uncooked state.

Ranunculus aquatilis var. *hispidulus* — Water Buttercup. Stems submersed in water; lvs finely divided threads; fls with 5 white petals. Common in shallow ponds below 6500. SL. April–July.

R. alismaefolius var. *hartwegii* — Western Plantain Buttercup. Fig. 10. Stem 3–8 dm, with lanceolate lvs 4–12 cm long; fl with 5 bright yellow petals. Widespread. MM, MCF, S, A. May–July.

One of the first wildflowers to appear in soggy fields after snow melts.

R. orthorhynchus var. *hallii*—Straight-beaked Buttercup. Fig. 11. Stem 1.5–5 dm tall with pinnately compound lvs; fl with 5 petals, bright yellow underneath and dull yellow above; seeds with straight beak. Wet meadows below 7000. MCF, MM. May–July.

R. eschscholtzii var. *oxynotus*—Eschscholtz's Butter-

Fig. 11 *Ranunculus orthorhynchus*   Fig. 12 *Ranunculus esch-scholtzii*

cup. Fig. 12. Lower lvs deeply 3–parted; fl with 5 yellow petals. Frequent on open rocky slopes, 8000–14000. S, A. July–Aug.

Eschscholtz was a naturalist on an early Russian scientific expedition that explored the West Coast.

R. occidentalis var. *eisenii*—Western Buttercup. Stems erect, wiry, 2–7 dm tall; lower lvs 3–parted; fl with 5–6 yellow petals. Common in dryish semishade at middle altitudes or lower. FW, C, MCF. April–July.

R. californicus—California Buttercup. Fig. 13. Stem erect, 3–6 dm tall; lower lvs pinnate or occasionally 3–parted; fl with 9–16 petals. Below 3000, Kaweah River to American River on w. slope. FW. Feb–May.

R. hystriculus—Waterfall Buttercup. Pl. 1g. Stem 1.5–

Fig. 13 *Ranunculus californicus*

4 dm tall; lower lvs with 3 shallow lobes; fl with 5 white sepals and 8–12 cream to yellowish petals. Among wet rocks, particularly near waterfalls. West slope, 3000–6000, especially Yosemite. FW, MCF. April–June.

R. flammula var. *ovalis*—Creeping Buttercup. Fig. 14. Stems creeping, rooting where touching soil; lvs linear. Marshy ground below 7500, frequent in Yosemite. MM. July–Aug.

R. muricatus—Prickle-seeded Buttercup. Pl. 1*f*. Stems low or creeping; lvs rounded to kidney-shaped, fleshy; fl with 5 yellow petals; seeds in a rounded cluster, each with many curved spines. Wet places below 4000. FW, MCF. April–May.

Introduced from Europe.

Fig. 14 *Ranunculus flammula*

Genus *Thalictrum*

Thalictrum fendleri — Fendler's Meadow Rue. Pl. 2*e*. Stem 3–8 dm tall; fls are all either male or female on any one plant, no petals present. Moist soil near streams, widespread, 3000–10000. MCF, MM, S. May–Aug.

Indians used the roots to make a tea to cure colds and venereal disease, and they made shampoo from the powdered dried roots.

FAMILY PAEONIACEAE (PEONY)

Paeonia brownii—Wild Peony. Pl. 2*a*. Stems several, 2–4 dm tall; lvs divided 3 times, with bluish waxy surface; fl single, maroon, hanging downward. Dry open areas of forest, 4000–8000, Tuolumne Co. north. MCF. April–June.

Indians made a curative tea for lung trouble from the leaves.

FAMILY NYMPHAEACEAE (WATER LILY)

Nuphar polysepalum — Yellow Pond Lily. Lvs large, floating; fls yellow; easily recognized. Ponds, Yosemite north. SL. April–Sept.

Indians boiled or roasted the roots for stews or ground them into flour, and they ate the seeds roasted like popcorn. The Pond Lily is an important food for water birds.

KEY TO THE FAMILY MALVACEAE (HOLLYHOCK)

1a—Lvs round to heart-shaped. *Malva parviflora.*
1b—Lvs divided or lobed. See 2.

2a—Whitish waxy covering on stem. *Sidalcea glaucescens.*
2b—Stem without waxy covering. See 3.

3a—Fls crowded along spike. See 4.
3b—Fls loosely spaced along spike. See 5.

4a—West of Sierra crest. *S. ranunculacea.*
4b—East of Sierra crest. *S. oregana.*

5a—Stems trailing, very hairy. *S. reptans.*
5b—Stems erect, slightly hairy. *S. malvaeflora.*

Many species in the hollyhock family are important food sources for the caterpillars of the West Coast Lady, Hair Streaks, and Skipper butterflies.

Genus *Malva*

Malva parviflora — Cheeseweed. Stems erect, 3–8 dm tall; lvs many, dark green, roundish; fls small, white-pink. Frequent in disturbed places. FW, MCF. Flowers most of year.

Introduced from Europe.

Genus *Sidalcea*

Sidalcea glaucescens—Glaucous Sidalcea. Stem 5–8 dm tall with whitish waxy covering; lower lvs deeply 5–7-lobed; fls pinkish. Dry slopes in forest openings, 3000–11000. MCF. May–July.

S. *ranunculacea*—Marsh Sidalcea. Creeping rootstock rooting at intervals; stem 2–5 dm tall; lower lvs shallowly 5-lobed, upper 5–7-parted; many fls pinkish, crowded together. Wet stream banks and meadows, 6000–9000, Kern and Tulare Cos. MCF. July–Aug.

S. *oregana* subsp. *spicata*—Spiked Sidalcea. Stem 3–6 dm tall; lower lvs 3–5-toothed, upper palmately 5–7-lobed; fls dense pinkish spikes. Dry open forest areas along e. slope. MCF. June–Aug.

S. *reptans*—Creeping Sidalcea. Rootstalk rooting at intervals; plant 2–5 dm tall; all lvs shallowly 5–7-lobed; fls few, loosely spaced along spike. Wet meadows, 4000–8000. MM. July–Aug.

S. *malvaeflora* subsp. *asprella*—Harsh Sidalcea. Fig. 15. Stem 1.5–6 dm tall; lvs deeply divided, 5–7 lobes; fls pinkish, loosely spaced. Dry open areas below 4000 on w. slope. FW, MCF. May–July.

FAMILY SARRACENIACEAE (PITCHER PLANT)

Darlingtonia californica — California Pitcher Plant or Cobra Lily. Fig. 16. Lvs yellowish-green, 2–6 dm tall, formed into rounded tubes, enlarged at top so as to resemble the head of a raised cobra. Bogs at 6000–7000, northern Sierra. MCF. May–June.

Interior of the tubular leaf is lined with downward pointing hairs that trap insects, which provide a nitrogen source for the plant. Rare, do not pick!

FAMILY DROSERACEAE (SUNDEW)

Drosera rotundifolia—Sundew Plant. Fig. 17. Plant is

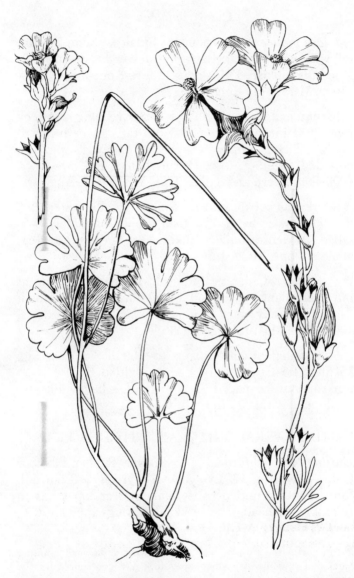

Fig. 15 *Sidalcea malvaeflora*

small flat rosette of lvs; lvs 2–6 cm long, round with
many reddish hairs; fls small, white. Cold and mossy

Fig. 16 *Darlingtonia californica*   Fig. 17 *Drosera rotundi-folia*

swamps below 8000, widespread. MCF. July–Aug.

The hairs on the leaves exude a sticky fluid to trap and digest insects for their nitrogen content.

KEY TO THE FAMILY GERANIACEAE
(GERANIUM)

1a—Lvs elongate, variously cut. See 2.
1b—Lvs rounded, palmately divided. See 3.

2a—Lvs partly divided. *Erodium botrys.*
2b—Lvs completely divided into lobes. *E. cicutarium.*

3a—Petals 2–9 mm long. See 4.
3b—Petals 11–21 mm long. See 5.

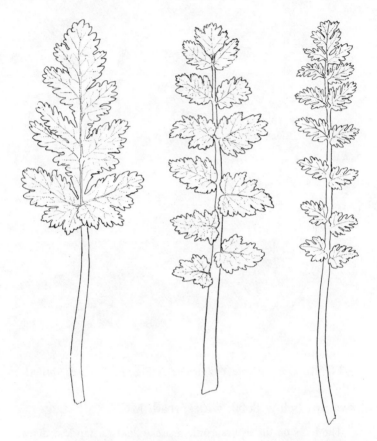

Fig. 18*a, Erodium botrys; b, Erodium moschatum; c, Erodium cicutarium*

4a—Petals purple. *Geranium dissectum.*
4b—Petals pale rose or white. *G. carolinianum.*

5a—Petals white. *G. richardsonii.*
5b—Petals rose. *G. californicum.*

Many of the species in the geranium family are an important food source for cattle, as well as for 17 bird species, rabbits, rodents, deer, and the caterpillar of the Dainty Yellow Butterfly. The young leaves of species in the genus *Erodium* can be eaten by humans raw in salads or cooked as greens.

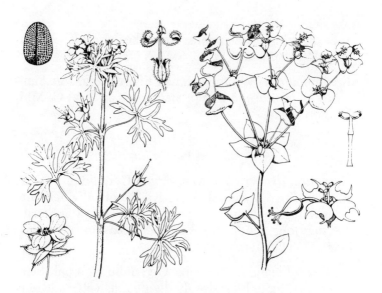

Fig. 19 *Geranium dissectum*   Fig. 20 *Euphorbia crenulata*

Genus *Erodium* (Storksbill)

The *Erodium* seed has a long tail that dries into a coil resembling a clock spring. At night the tail straightens when moistened by dew but it re-coils in the morning when dried by the sun. The sharp-pointed seed thus slowly plants itself by the repeated straightening and coiling of the tail. You can simulate dew by breathing heavily on a well-coiled seed. If you then place it in a hot sunny place, it will coil before your eyes. A favorite children's pastime is to push one of the long needlelike seed pods through another to made a pair of "scissors."

The *Erodiums* were accidentally introduced into California by the Spaniards during the mission period, because the seeds clung to the wool of sheep brought from the Mediterranean countries.

Erodium botrys—Long-beaked Filaree. Fig. 18*a*. Plant low to ground; lvs elongate and partly pinatified; fls with purple petals; style (beak or tail) 9–12 mm long. Common and widespread, mostly at lower elevations. FW, C, MCF, MM, SS. March–June.

E. cicutarium—Red-stemmed Filaree. Fig. 18*c*. Plant low to ground; stems reddish; lvs elongate and finely pinnatified, short dense hairs give lf a whitish appearance; fls with purple petals; style (beak or tail) 2–4 cm long. Widespread. FW, C, MM, SS. Feb.–May.

E. moschatum—White-stemmed Filaree. Fig. 18*b*. Similar to *E. cicutarium* except stem whitish. FW, C, MM, SS. Feb.–May.

Genus *Geranium*

Geranium dissectum — Cut-leaved Geranium. Fig. 19. Annual. Stem weak, slender; lvs deeply divided into narrow segments; purple petals same length as sepals, 7–8 mm long. Widespread in open areas, mostly below 3000. FW, C. March–June.

G. carolinianum—Carolina Geranium. Annual. Stem erect, 2–4 dm tall; lvs deeply divided; fls with pale pink to white petals same length as sepals, 5–8 mm. Common in shady places below 5000. FW, C, MCF. April–July.

G. richardsonii—Richardson's Geranium. Fig. 21. Perennial. Stem erect, 2.5–9 dm tall; lvs partly 5–7-lobed; fls with white purple-veined petals, 10–18 mm longer than sepals. Moist places, 4000–9000. MCF, MM. July–Aug.

G. californicum — California Geranium. Perennial. Stem 2–6 dm tall; lvs 5–7-parted; fls with rose-pink or white petals with dark veins, 12–21 mm, nearly twice the length of sepals. Moist places, 4000–8000, Tuolumne Co. and south. MCF, MM. June–July.

FAMILY LIMNANTHACEAE (MEADOW FOAM)

Limnanthes alba — White Meadow Foam. Pl. 2*b*. Lvs narrowly divided 1 or 2 times; fls creamy-white. FW. April–June.

Masses of flowers are a common sight in low wet meadows or stream bottoms of western foothills.

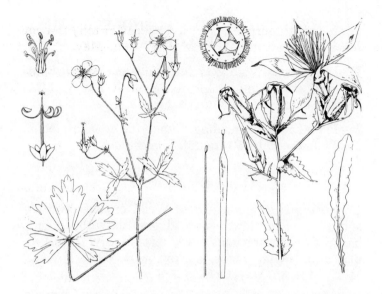

Fig. 21 *Geranium richardsonii*   Fig. 22 *Mentzelia laevicaulis*

KEY TO THE FAMILY LINACEAE (FLAX)

1a—Fls blue. *Linum perenne.*
1b—Fls white to pinkish. *Hesperolinon micranthum.*

Genus *Linum*

Linum perenne subsp. *lewisii*—Western Blue Flax. Perennial. Stems 2–6 dm tall; lvs linear, 1–2 cm long; fls light blue. Dry open ridges, 1400–12000, widespread. MCF, MM, S, A. May–Sept.

Seeds contain a cyanide compound, but Indians deactivated the poison by roasting and then ate the seeds. They also steeped the root to make an eye medicine.

Genus *Hesperolinon*

Hesperolinon micranthum — Small-flowered Flax. Annual. Plant tiny with slender, threadlike stems, 1–4 dm tall; fls pale pink to white, 2–3 mm long. Often found on dry, open, serpentine rocks of western foothills, 1000–5000. FW, MCF. May–July.

[35]

KEY TO THE FAMILY EUPHORBIACEAE
(SPURGE)

1a—Lvs covered with gray feltlike hairs. *Eremocarpus setigerus.*

1b—Lvs hairless, yellow-green. See 2.

2a—Plant flat and spreading. *Euphorbia albomarginata.*

2b—Plant erect, 12–50 cm tall. *E. crenulata.*

Genus *Eremocarpus*

Eremocarpus setigerus—Dove Weed or Turkey Mullein. Pl. 2c. Plant low; lvs broad, grayish, with stinging hairs; fls inconspicuous. Frequent in dry disturbed places and along roads, mostly below 6000. FW, C, MCF, MM, SS. May–Oct.

An important food plant of doves and quail. Indians used the crushed leaves to stun fish.

Genus *Euphorbia*

Euphorbia albomarginata — Rattlesnake Weed. Plant flat, spreading over ground; stem contains white milky juice; fls numerous, small, 1.5–2 mm wide, round, white. Frequent in dry disturbed places. FW, MCF, PJ, SS. All year.

Indians applied the crushed plant to open rattlesnake bites.

E. crenulata—Chinese Caps. Fig. 20. Stem hairless, somewhat waxy, 12–50 cm tall; lvs ovate; fl actually a large yellow-green cape of lvs surrounding petal-less fls. Common in semi-shaded dry places below 5000. FW, MCF. March–Aug.

KEY TO THE FAMILY LOASACEAE (LOASA)

1a—Petals 5–8 cm long. *Mentzelia laevicaulis.*

1b—Petals 0.4–0.5 cm long. *M. congesta.*

Genus *Mentzelia*

Mentzelia laevicaulis — Blazing Star. Fig. 22. Stems stout, 3–10 dm tall; lvs lanceolate with wavy margins; fls with large yellow petals and many yellow stamens. Dry disturbed places below 9500. FW, MCF, PJ. June–Oct.

M. congesta—Ventana Stick Leaf. Stem 1–4 dm tall; lvs lanceolate with wavy margins; fls with pale yellow petals, orange at base, 4–5 mm long. Common in loose disturbed soil below 9000. MCF, PJ. May–July.

KEY TO THE FAMILY VIOLACEAE (VIOLET)

1a—Fls with some yellow, dry habitat. See 2.
1b—Fls without any yellow, moist habitat. See 7.

2a—Lf blade divided, cut, or lobed. See 3.
2b—Lf blade not cut or lobed. See 4.

3a—Lf divided, 3–9 fingerlike lobes. *Viola lobata.*
3b—Lf divided into 3 large lobes which are further sub-divided. *V. sheltonii.*

4a—Plants white, wooly. *V. tomentosa.*
4b—Plants not white, wooly. See 5.

5a—Fls deep yellow, lvs heart-shaped. *V. glabella.*
5b—Fls pale yellow, lvs longer than wide. See 6.

6a—Lvs oblong, ovary hairless. *V. bakeri.*
6b—Lvs ovate, ovary hairy. *V. purpurea.*

7a—Fls white. *V. macloskeyi.*
7b—Fls blue-violet. *V. adunca.*

Stems and leaves of violets are edible when cooked as greens or when candied. Doves, quail, grouse, rabbits and small rodents eat the seeds, and the leaves are important food of fritillary butterfly caterpillars.

Genus *Viola*

Viola lobata—Pine Violet. Fig. 23. Lvs 3–8 cm wide,

Fig. 23 *Viola lobata*   Fig. 24 *Viola purpurea*

deeply lobed; fls yellow with bronze backs. Dry slopes in forest openings of w. slope at mid-elevations. MCF. April–July.

V. *sheltonii*—Fan Violet. Lvs 3–5 cm wide with 3 main fingerlike lobes which are further subdivided; fls yellow, veined with brownish purple. Semi-shade in rich loam, w. slope 2500–8000. April–July.

V. *tomentosa*—Wooly Violet. Entire plant covered by gray wooly hairs; fls yellow with purple markings on backs. Dry rocky places, 5000–6500, northern Sierra. MCF, PJ. June–Aug.

V. *glabella*—Smooth, Stream, or Pioneer Violet. Pl. 2*f*. Lvs heart-shaped, 3–8 cm wide; fls pale yellow, backs of middle and lower petals purple veined. Damp stream banks and shady places below 8000. MCF. March–July.

V. *bakeri*—Baker's Violet. Lvs oblong-lanceolate, 2.5–3.5 cm long; fls pale yellow with some purple on back

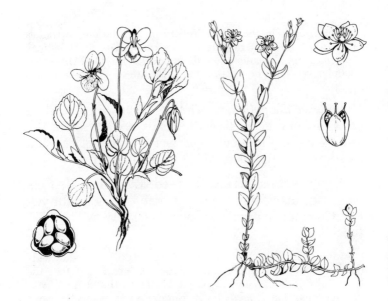

Fig. 25 *Viola adunca*   Fig. 26 *Hypericum anagalloides*

of lower petals only. Open areas in forest shortly after snow melts, w. slope 4500–8000. MCF. May–July.

V. purpurea—Mountain Violet. Fig. 24. Lvs narrowly ovate, 2–4 cm long; fls yellow with purple on backs of petals. Dry open slopes 2000–6000, w. slope. MCF. April–June.

V. macloskeyi—Macloskey's Violet. Stems creeping; fls white with some purple veins in lower petals. Wet meadows and along streams, 3500–11000. MM. May–Aug.

V. adunca—Western Dog Violet. Fig. 25. Fls violet to blue. Damp places, common entire w. slope. FW, MCF. March–June.

FAMILY HYPERICACEAE (ST. JOHN'S WORT)
Key to the Genus *Hypericum*

1a—Low matlike plant. *Hypericum anagalloides*.
1b—Tall, wiry stemmed plants. *H. perforatum*.

Some species in the genus *Hypericum* can become a serious problem as weeds in rangeland. The caterpillars of Hairstreak Butterflies are dependent on these species for food, however. Globular swellings or galls on the stalks are caused by a midge insect.

Hypericum anagalloides—Tinker's Penny. Fig. 26. Plant grows in low mats; fls with sepals and petals nearly same length. Frequent near wet springy places and meadows. 4000–10000. MCF, MM. June–Aug.

H. perforatum—Klamath Weed. Lvs linear, 1–3 cm long with many tiny black perforations; fls bright yellow. Common in dry fields below 5000. FW, MM, MCF. June–Sept.

In the past this species covered thousands of acres and made the land unuseable for grazing cattle. In was found that the beautiful metallic green and purple beetles of the genus *Chysolina* feed only on *Hypericum* in Europe, so these beetles were brought to the West Coast. They have proved to be an effective biological control of Klamath Weed.

KEY TO THE FAMILY PAPAVERACEAE (POPPY)

1a—Fls white or cream. See 2.
1b—Fls orange. See 3.

2a—Lvs opposite, plants low. *Platystemon californicus*.
2b—Lvs alternate, plants spiny. *Argemone munita*.

3a—Orange fls with a purple spot. *Stylomecon*.
3b—Orange fls without purple spot. *Eschscholzia*.

Genus *Platystemon*

Platystemon californicus — Cream Cups. Fig. 27. Lvs linear, 5–8 cm long, opposite; fls cream with or without a yellow dot at base; sap milky. Lower w. slope. FW, MCF, MM. March–June.

A spring flower that gives open meadows a massive cream color.

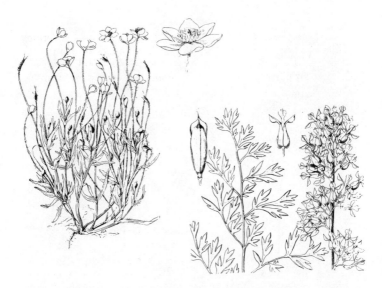

Fig. 27 *Platystemon californicus*   Fig. 28 *Dicentra chrysan-tha*

Genus *Argemone*

Argemone munita subsp. *rotundata*—Prickly Poppy. Pl. 2g. Stems with prickly yellow spines, 6–15 dm tall; lvs stout; fls large, white, with orange stamens. Common in dry disturbed places, especially roadsides. FW, C, MCF, SS, PJ. April–July.

Genus *Stylomecon*

Stylomecon heterophylla—Wind Poppy. Lvs divided; fls with orange-red petals having a large purple spot, surrounded by green, at base. Open grassy places, Mariposa Co. and south at lower elevations. FW, C. April–May.

Genus *Eschscholzia*

Eschscholzia californica — California Poppy. Lvs divided into many linear segments; fls with shiny orange to light yellow petals. Common in open dry places below 7000. FW, MCF, MM. April–Aug.

Official California state flower. Seeds are food for some birds. Indians used the leaves to relieve the pain of toothache.

[41]

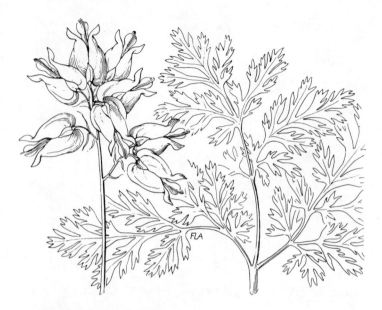

Fig. 29 *Dicentra formosa*

FAMILY FUMARIACEAE (FUMITORY)

Key to the Genus *Dicentra*

1a—Fls golden yellow. *Dicentra chrysantha.*
1b—Fls rose to whitish. See 2.

2a—Two or more fls per stem. *D. formosa.*
2b—One fl per stem. *D. uniflora.*

Dicentra chrysantha—Golden Ear Drops. Fig. 28. Lvs divided into linear lobes; fls bright yellow, flattened in elongated heart-shape. Common in areas of recent fires and other disturbed places. Dry slopes below 5000 on w. slope. FW, MCF. April–Sept.

D. formosa — Bleeding Heart. Fig. 29. Lvs lacy; fls rose-purple, flattened in elongated heart-shape. Frequent in damp, shady woods below 7000 on w. slope. MCF. March–July.

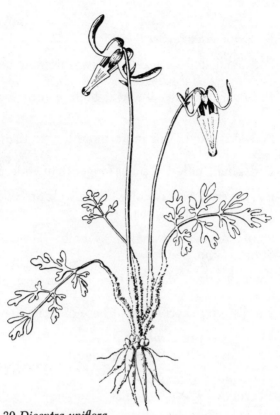

Fig. 30 *Dicentra uniflora*

D. uniflora—Steer's Head. Fig. 30. Plant low, 5–10 cm tall; fls white to pink, flattened in elongated heart-shape with two large reflexed sepals which give fls appearance of a Texas Longhorn cow, 1 fl per stem. Rocky places, 1500–10000, Yosemite north. MCF, S. May–July.

To be looked for where snow has recently melted.

KEY TO THE FAMILY CRUCIFERAE
(MUSTARD)

1a—Growing in slow moving streams. *Rorippa.*
1b—Not growing directly in water. See 2.

2a—Pods round, dislike. *Thysanocarpus.*

[43]

2b—Pods not disclike. See 3.

3a—Pod elongated with definite constrictions between each seed. *Rahpanus*.

3b—Pods various but without definite contrictions. See 4.

4a—Pod elongated, 3 or more times longer than wide. See 5.

4b—Pods small, only 1–2 times longer than wide. See 15.

5a—Lvs covered with definite bluish wax. *Streptanthus*.

5b—Lvs without bluish wax. See 6.

6a—Stems somewhat 4-angled, fls white. *Barbarea*.

6b—Stems round. See 7.

7a—Distinct whorl of lvs at base of stem near ground. See 8.

7b—No distinct whorl of lvs at base of stem. See 10.

8a—Lf edges entire. *Arabis*.

8b—Lf edges toothed or divided. See 9.

9a—Fls white. *Cardamine*.

9b—Fls yellow. *Thelypodium*.

10a—Long pods without apparent seam, fls yellow. *Brassica*.

10b—Pods with seams, opening at maturity. See 11.

11a—Fls white to purple. See 12.

11b—Fls yellow or orange. See 14.

```
1 millimeter
10 millimeters = 1 centimeter = 13/32 inch
10 centimeters = 1 decimeter = ca. 4 inches
10 decimeters = 1 meter = 3.3 feet
```

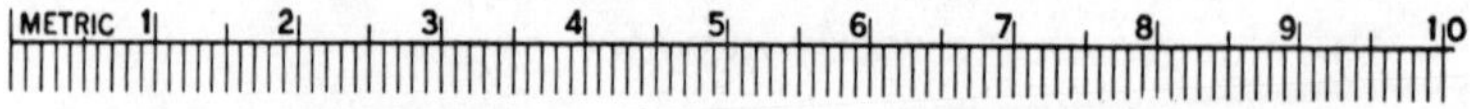

Fig. 31 Metric scale 1:1

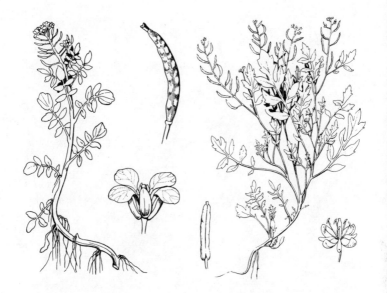

Fig. 32 *Rorippa nasturtium-aquaticum*   Fig. 33 *Rorippa curvisiliqua*

12a—Lvs simple, dry places. *Arabis.*
12b—Lvs pinnate, damp places. See 13.

13a—Lower stem leafless. *Dentaria.*
13b—Lower stem leafy. *Cardamine.*

14a—Lvs entire, linear. *Erysimum.*
14b—Lvs pinnate. *Descurainia.*

15a—Pods triangular, notched at top. *Capsella.*
15b—Pods linear. See 16.

16a—Pods with seam along edge. *Draba.*
16b—Pods with seam down center of pod. *Lepidium.*

The mustard family contains a variety of interesting seed-pod shapes, each of which can present a challenge to a photographer. Identification of species in this family is easiest when some of the oldest seed pods are obtained with the flowers and leaves.

Key to the Genus *Rorippa* (Water Cress)

1a—Flowers white. *Rorippa nasturtium-aquaticum.*
1b—Flowers yellow. *R. curvisiliqua.*

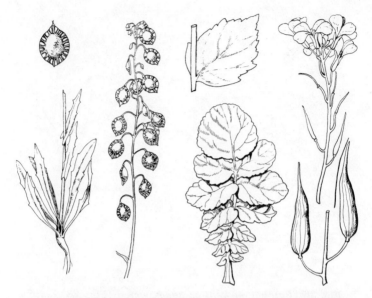

Fig. 34 *Thysanocarpus curvipes*   Fig. 35 *Raphanus sativus*

Rorippa nasturtium-aquaticum—White Water Cress.
Fig. 32. Stems much-branched and sprawling; lvs pinnate 1–10 cm long; fls small, white; seed pod curving.
Found in shallow, slow-flowing streams. Common below 8000. FW, MCF, MM. All year.

Originally this species was introduced for cultivation for salad use, but it now grows wild.

R. curvisiliqua—Yellow Water Cress. Fig. 33. Stems much branched, 1–3 dm tall; lvs pinnatified, 2–8 cm long; fls yellow; seed pod curved. Common in shallow slow-moving streams below 10000. FW, MCF, MM. April–Sept.

Genus *Thysanocarpus*

Thysanocarpus curvipes—Fringe Pod or Lace Pod. Fig. 34. Stem slender, branched, 2–5 dm tall; fls tiny, white; pod distinctive, flat, single-seeded, with a thin papery margin on curved pedicels. Common in open grassy places below 5000 on w. slope. FW, MCF. March–May.

[46]

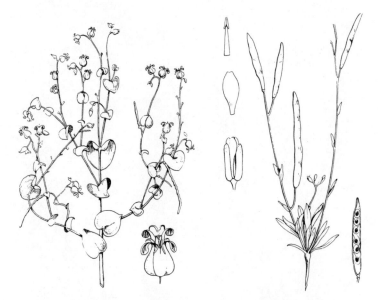

Fig. 36 *Streptanthus tortuosus*   Fig. 37 *Arabis platysperma*

Genus *Raphanus*

Raphanus sativus—Wild Radish. Fig. 35. Stem 3–12 dm tall; lower lvs pinnately parted; fls white to rose or yellow; pod cylindrical and not split, constricted between each seed. Common in disturbed places. FW, C, MCF. Feb.–May.

Although the wild radish is related to the garden radish, the root is not edible.

Genus *Streptanthus*

Streptanthus tortuosus — Mountain Jewel Flower. Fig. 36. Entire plant hairless and covered with bluish waxy bloom; stem 2–10 dm tall; yellow-green, heart-shaped or rounded, attached to stem between lower lobes of leaf; fls purplish to yellowish. Dry rocky places, 1000–12000, very common. FW, C, MCF. April–Sept.

Key to the Genus *Arabis* (Rock Cress)

1a—Pods 3–8 mm wide. See 2.
1b—Pods normally less than 3 mm wide. See 4.

[47]

Fig. 38 *Arabis glaucovalvula*   Fig. 39 *Arabis rectissima*

2a—Pods bent downward. See 3.
2b—Pods erect or bent upward. *A. platysperma.*

3a—Lvs with dense white hair, pod pointed downward. *A glauco-valvula.*
3b—Lvs without dense hair, pod curved downward. *A. repanda.*

4a—Basal lvs obovate, waxy surface. *A. glabra.*
4b—Basal lvs linear, not waxy. See 5.

5a—Pods ascending from stem. See 6.
5b—Pods at right angles or bent downward from stem. See 10.

6a—Lower lvs felt gray. See 7.
6b—Lower lvs greenish, but with hairs. See 8.

7a—Basal lvs 3–10 cm long, pod 6–12 cm long. *A. sparsiflora.*
7b—Basal lvs 2–3 cm long, pods 4–6 cm long. *A. inyoensis.*

8a—Pods and pedicels erect, fls white. *A. drummondii.*
8b—Pods and pedicels slightly bent in becoming erect, fls pink.
    See 9.

[48]

9a—Plants less than 3 dm tall. *A. lyallii.*
9b—Plants more than 3 dm tall. *A. divaricarpa.*

10a—Basal lvs with large hairs along margins. *A. rectissima.*
10b—Basal lvs without margin hairs. See 11.

11a—Pedicels 2–4 mm long, lvs mostly hairless. *A. lemmonii.*
11b—Pedicels 6–20 mm long, lvs hairy. See 12.

12a—Margins of upper stem lvs rolled downward. *A. holboellii.*
12b—Margins of lvs not rolled as above. See 13.

13a—Basal lvs with entire margins. *A. inyoensis.*
13b—Basal lvs with toothed margins. See 14.

14a—Pods 4–6 cm long. *A. perennans.*
14b—Pods 6–12 cm long, w. side of Sierra. *A. sparsiflora.*

Species in the large rock cress genus have small flowers that quickly become long narrow seed pods, attached at various angles. Orange Tip, Marble, and White butterfly caterpillars feed on plants of this genus. The botanical name comes from the Greek word for Arabia.

Arabis platysperma—Broad-seeded Rock Cress. Fig. 37. Stem 1–4 dm tall; lvs many, basal oblanceolate, greenish, 2–5 cm long; fls pink to white; pods erect, 3–7 cm long, seeds 3–4 mm wide. Dry rocky places, 5500–12000, common. MCF, S, A. June–Aug.

A. glaucovalvula—Blue-podded Rock Cress. Fig. 38. Stem 1.5–4 dm tall; lvs lanceolate with dense white hairs; fls whitish to pink; pods oblong, 2–4 cm long, pointed downward. Dry rocky places. SS, PJ. March–May.

A. repanda—Repand Rock Cress. Stem 2–8 dm tall; lvs obovate-broadly oblanceolate, 1–3 cm long; fls white to pinkish; pods 4–10 cm long, curved downward. Dry slopes, 4500–12000. MCF, S. June–Aug.

A. glabra—Tower Mustard. Pl. 2d. Stem distinctive, unbranched, 4–12 dm tall; upper lvs arrowhead-shaped, surface blue, wax-like; fls yellow; pods 4–10 cm long. Semi-shade areas of w. slope below 7000, very common. FW, C, MCF. March–July.

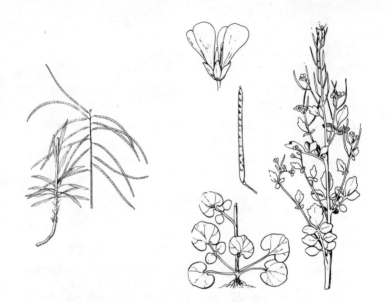

Fig. 40 *Arabis holboelli*   Fig. 41 *Cardamine breweri*

A. inyoensis—Inyo Rock Cress. Stem 2–5 dm tall; lvs felt gray, 2–3 cm long; fls pink to purplish; pods ascending 4–6 cm long and 2 mm wide. Dry rocky places, 5000–11000 on e. slope. MCF, PJ. May–July.

A. drummondii — Drummond's Rock Cress. (See p. 22.) Stem 3–9 dm tall; lower lvs oblanceolate, 2–7 cm long; fls white to pinkish; pods many, crowded together, erect, 4–10 cm long. 5500–11000, e. of main crest. MCF, S, PJ. June–July.

A. lyallii—Lyall's Rock Cress. Plant is a cushion of lvs with slender stems, 4–25 cm tall; lvs 1–3 cm long; fls rose to purple; pods erect 3–5 cm long. Open rocky places 8000–12000. S, A. July–Aug.

Named for Sir Charles Lyall, a prominent paleogeologist who was a close friend of Charles Darwin.

A. divaricarpa—Bent-pod Rock Cress. Stem very tall, 3–9 dm; lvs loosely hairy; fls pink to purplish; pods slightly bent upward, 2–8 cm long. Dry slopes under shade of pines, 7000–11000 on e. slope. PJ, MCF. July–Aug.

[50]

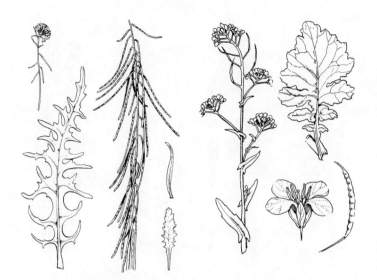

Fig. 42 *Thelypodium lasiophyllum*   Fig. 43 *Brassica campestris*

A. *rectissima* — Bristly-leaved Rock Cress. Fig. 39. Stems 2–8 dm tall; basal lvs 1–3 cm long with large coarse hairs along margins; fls white to pinkish; fls and pods pointing downward. Dry rock slopes, 4000–9000, common. MCF. June–July.

A. *lemmonii* — Lemmon's Rock Cress. (See p. 63.) Stem 6–20 cm tall; lvs oblanceolate, 1–2 cm long; pedicels 2–4 mm long; fls pink to purple; pods horizontal or descending, 2–4 cm long. Dry rocky places, 8000–14000, throughout high country. MCF, S, A. June–Aug.

A. *holboelli* var. *retrofracta*—Holboell's Rock Cress. Fig. 40. Stem 2–8 cm tall, densely hairy; lvs greenish, feltlike, 1–5 cm long, upper leaf margin rolled downward; fls pink to white; pods erect, 3.5–8 cm long. Dry rocky places, 6000–11000, common. MCF, S. May–July.

A. *perennans*—Perennial Rock Cress. Pl. 3*a*. Stem 1.5–6 dm tall; lvs oblanceolate and toothed; fls purplish; pods curved downward. FW, MCF. April–July.

[51]

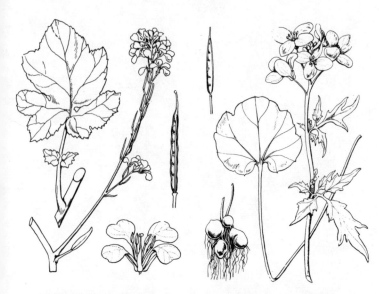

Fig. 44 *Brassica nigra*   Fig. 45 *Dentaria californica*

Genus *Caramine*

Cardamine breweri — Brewer's Bitter Cress. Fig. 41. Stem 2–6 dm tall; stem lvs pinnate with 3–5 oblong leaflets; fls white; pods ascending, 1.5–2.5 cm long. Wet shady places along streams, 4000–10500, widespread. MCF, S. May–July.

Named for William Brewer who headed the first state surveying party to explore California.

Genus *Thelypodium*

Thelypodium lasiophyllum — California Mustard. Fig. 42. Stem branched, 2–10 dm tall; lvs irregularly pinnate; fls many, pale yellowish-white. Common in disturbed areas. FW, MCF. March–July.

Genus *Barbarea*

Barbarea orthoceras — American Winter Cress. Stems stout, 2–4 dm tall; lvs pinnatified; fls pale yellow; pods ascending, 3–4.5 cm long. Springs, wet banks, meadows, 2500–11000, widespread. FW, MCF, MM, S. May–Sept.

Key to the Genus *Brassica* (Mustard)

1a—Upper lf bases clasping stem. *B. campestris.*
1b—Upper lf bases not clasping stem. See 2.

2a—Petals 7–8 mm long. *B. nigra.*
2b—Petals 5–6 mm long. *B. geniculata.*

Young mustard leaves can be cooked as greens, but the seeds should not be eaten; livestock have been poisoned by mustard seeds. Doves, finches, larks, rabbits, squirrels, deer and the White Butterflies use the mustards for food. All species in the genus originated in Europe.

Brassica campestris—Field Mustard. Fig. 43. Stem 3–12 dm tall; entire plant hairless and covered with blue waxy bloom; lower lvs 1–2 dm long, deeply lobed; fls yellow; pods stout, cylindrical, 2–5 cm long, with beak on end. Common. FW, C, MCF. Jan.–May.

B. nigra—Black Mustard. Fig. 44. Stem 5–25 dm tall, slightly hairy; lower lvs 1–2 dm long, deeply pinnatified with 1 large terminal lobe; fls bright yellow; cylindrical pods 1–2 cm long. Common on dry slopes. FW, C, MCF. April–July.

B. geniculata—Short-podded Mustard. Stem 4–8 dm tall; entire plant covered with feltlike white hairs; lower lvs 0.4–1 dm long and comblike; fls light yellow; pod thin cylindrical, 0.8–1.2 cm long, 1-seeded. Widespread. FW, C, MCF, MM, SS. May–Oct.

Key to the Genus *Dentaria* (Milkmaids)

1a—Basal lvs entire. *D. pachystigma.*
1b—Basal lvs divided. *D. californica.*

Dentaria pachystigma—Stout-beaked Toothwort. Stem 1.5–3 dm tall; stem lvs heart-shaped, fls pink. Cool shady woods, 5000–9500, w. slope. MCF. May–June.

D. californica—California Milkmaids. Fig. 45. Stem 1–4 dm tall; stem lvs 3–4-parted; fls white to pale rose. Shady woods, mostly below 3000 on w. slope. FW, C. Feb.–May.

[53]

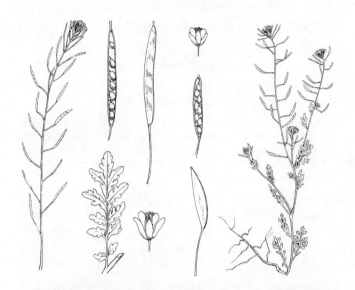

Fig. 46 *Descurainia richardsonii*   Fig. 47 *Descurainia pinnata*

Key to the Genus *Erysimum* (Wallflower)

1a—Stem 2–30 cm tall, fls yellow. *E. perenne.*
1b—Stem 20–100 cm tall, fls orange. *E. capitatum.*

Erysimum perenne—Sierra Wallflower. Pl. 3*b*. Stem 2–30 cm tall, greenish; fls bright yellow. Dry areas mostly above 7000, common. MCF, S, PJ. June–Aug.

E. capitatum—Douglas's Wallflower. Stem stout, 2–8 dm tall; lvs and stem light gray; fls usually orange but vary to yellow. Dry rocky places below 8000, common. FW, C, MCF. March–July.

Named for David Douglas, first trained botanist to explore the West Coast. In the early 1800s he wandered throughout the region with his Scotty dog. The Indians didn't molest him because they thought he was insane to be collecting and drying plants of little use to humans.

Key to the Genus *Descurainia* (Tansy Mustard)

1a—One row of seeds in the pod. *D. richardsonii.*
1b—Two rows of seed in the pod. *D. pinnata*

Plants of this lacy-leaved crucifer are common. Indians made flour from the seeds and steam-cooked the fresh plant, but even

[54]

Fig. 48 *Capsella bursa-pastoris*   Fig. 49 *Draba stenoloba*

after cooking it is very bitter. Seeds are an important food source for quail and other birds. Fresh plants cause blindness and tongue paralysis in cattle.

Descurainia richardsonii — Mountain Tansy Mustard. Fig. 46. Stem 4–8 dm tall; lvs pinnate; fls small, yellow, becoming many pods 8–15 mm long with 8–28 seeds, all in one row. Dry disturbed places, 4000–11000. MCF, MM. May–Aug.

D. pinnata subsp. *menziesii*—Sierra Tansy Mustard. Fig. 47. Stem 1–8 dm tall; lvs thin, pinnate; fls small, yellow, becoming many pods 5–12 mm long with 6–10 seeds in two rows. Dry slopes, 7000–11000. Mostly e. slope, common. MCF, PJ. May–Aug.

Genus *Capsella*

Capsella bursa-pastoris — Shepherd's Purse. Fig. 48. Stem branched, 2–5 dm tall; lvs pinnatified, mostly basal; fls small, white. Common in disturbed places below 7000. FW, C, MCF, MM, PJ, SS. All year.

Introduced from Europe. The flower pedicel resembles a purse string and the flattened seed pod a purse, much like that used by some European shepherds.

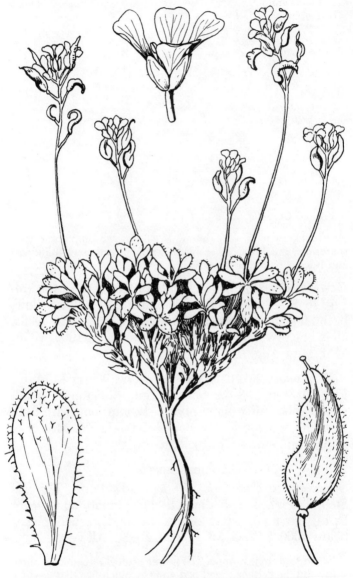

Fig. 50 *Draba lemmoni*

Key to the Genus *Draba*

1a—Plants annual, no sign of previous years growth. *D. stenoloba*.
1b—Perennials. See 2.

2a—Lvs hairless, all in basal rosette. See 3.
2b—Lvs hairy. See 4.

3a—Lvs hairy on both sides. *D. lemmonii*.
3b—Lvs with hairs on margins only. *D. densifolia*.

4a—Fls white. *D. breweri*.
4b—Fls yellow. See 5.

5a—Lvs 2–7 mm wide. *D. cruciata*.
5b—Lvs less than 2 mm wide. See 6.

6a—Lf margins with unbranched hairs. *D. paysonii*.
6b—Lf with branched hairs on margin. See 7.

7a—Flowering stem 1–3 cm tall. *D. sierrae*.
7b—Flowering stem 5–8 cm tall. *D. cruciata*.

Draba stenoloba var. *nana*—Alaska Whitlow Grass. Fig. 49. Annual. Plant 5–30 cm tall; lvs mostly basal, obovate, 1–4 cm long; 10–30 fls, yellowish; pod linear, 8–22 mm long. Damp shady places, 7000–12000. MCF, S, A. June–Aug.

D. lemmonii—Lemmon's Draba. Fig. 50 (See p. 63.) Plant cushionlike, spreading along ground; lvs oblanceolate, 5–20 mm long; stems leafless, 2–12 cm tall; fls yellow; pods flat, twisted. Common gravelly ridges, 8500–13000. A. July–Aug.

D. densifolia—Dense-leaved Draba. Plant tiny, cushionlike; lvs linear, 2–9 mm long, prominent hairs along margins, otherwise hairless; stem leafless, 1–12 cm; 3–15 fls, yellow; pods hairy, ovate, 2–7 mm long. Dry rocky places, 8500–13000, Tioga Pass and north. S, A. July–Aug.

D. breweri—Brewer's Whitlow Grass. Plant branching, cushionlike; lvs tufted, oblanceolate, 8–12 mm long, hairs grayish, 1–4 lvs on flowering stem; 10–25 fls, white; pods oblong and twisted. Rocky places, 8500–

13000, all high mountain crests. A. July–Aug.

Named for William Brewer, who was the leader of a team
that surveyed, explored, and mapped California for the first time.
His journal, *Up and Down California*, described California before there were roads or many towns.

D. cruciata—Cross-flowered Draba. Plant cushionlike
with many prostrate stems; lvs obovate, 5–12 mm long
with stiff forked hairs and stalked, star-branched hairs
on margins; fls yellow; pod lanceolate, 6–10 mm long.
Rocky places, 9000–12500, southern Sierra. A. July–
Aug..

D. paysonii var. *treleasii* – Payson's Draba. Pl. 3c.
Plant much-branched and matted; lvs dense, overlap-
ping, linear, 4–14 mm long, ca. 1 mm wide, margin
hairs mostly unbranched; fls light yellow; pod ovate.
Rocky places above 9000, Sonora Pass north. A. July–
Aug.

D. sierrae—Sierra Draba. Plant tiny, cushionlike; lvs
densely overlapping, grayish, 2–6 mm long, with hairs
on margins branched like a man's hair comb; stem leafless, 1–3 cm tall; fls yellow, pods ovate 3–8 mm long,
twisted. Dry scree 11000–13000, Mono Pass and south.
A. July–Aug.

Genus *Lepidum*

Lepidum densiflorum – Pepper Grass. Annual. Plant
small, branching, 3–5 dm tall; lvs oblanceolate, margins
variable from entire to toothed; fls minute; pods many,
rounded-ovate, 2.5 mm wide. Widespread, Yosemite.
FW, C, MCF. March–May.

KEY TO THE FAMILY CARYOPHYLLACEAE
(PINK)

1a—Sepals separate. See 2.
1b—Sepals united into a tubular calyx. See 5.
2a—Petal tips not lobed. See 3.
2b—Petal tips with 2 lobes. See 4.

3a—Styles as many as sepals. *Sagina saginoides.*
3b—Styles fewer than the sepals. *Arenaria.*

4a—Seed capsule elongated cylinder. *Cerastium.*
4b—Seed capsule oblong or ovoid. *Stellaria.*

5a—3 styles. *Silene.*
5b—2 styles. *Tunica.*

Genus *Sagina*

Sagina saginoides var. *hesperia* — Arctic Pearlwort. Plant low sprawling, hairless; lvs linear, 5–10 mm long; fls with tiny sepals and petals, 1–2 mm. Often seen in moist places, 4000–12000. FW, MCF, MM, S. May–Sept.

Key to the Genus *Arenaria* (Sandworts)

1a—Sepals with 3 green lines on back. *A. obtusiloba.*
1b—Sepals with 1 green line on back. *A. kingii.*

Arenaria obtusiloba—Alpine Sandwort. Plant compact, cushionlike; stems flowering, 1–6 dm tall; sepals with 3 green ribs; fls 6–7 mm long. Rocky slopes, 10500–13000, Tioga Pass and south. S, A. July–Aug.

A. *kingii* var. *glabrescens*—King's Smooth Sandwort. Pl. 3d. Plants 1–2 dm tall; sepal with 1 green rib, 3.5–4.5 mm long, white petals longer. Rocky places below 13000. MCF, S, A. June–Aug.

Key to the Genus *Cerastium* (Powder Horn)

1a—Found above 9000 ft. *C. beeringianum.*
1b—Found below 9000 ft. *C. vulgatum.*

Cerastium beeringianum — Alpine Cerastium. Plant matted with spreading stems, hairy; lvs oblong 7–20 mm; petals 6–8 mm. Near snowbanks in wet places above 9000. S, A. July–Aug.

C. *vulgatum*—Common Cerastium. Plant matted; stem hairy; lvs oblong, 1–2.5 cm; sepals and white petals 4–8 mm long. Common in lawns and elsewhere,

Fig. 51 *Stellaria jamesiana*   Fig. 52 *Stellaria longipes*

below 9000. FW, C, MCF. March–Aug.

Introduced from Europe.

Key to the Genus *Stellaria* (Chickweed or Starwort)

1a—Lvs ovate and with petiole. S. *media.*
1b—Lvs lanceolate, without petioles. See 2.

2a—Lvs 5–10 cm long. S. *jamesiana.*
2b—Lvs 1–3 cm long. See 3.

3a—Petals minute, shorter than sepals. S. *crispa.*
3b—Petals 3–5 mm long, sepals and petals same length. S. *longipes.*

The young shoot tips when boiled taste much like spinach. Doves, quail, some 20 other birds, the Cottontail Rabbit, and the Dainty Yellow Butterfly all feed on *Stellaria.*

[60]

Stellaria media — Common Chickweed. Pl. 3*f*. Stems weak, trailing along ground, with a single line of hairs along one side; lvs ovate, 1–3 cm long; sepals hairy. Very common in moist shady places. FW, C, MCF, MM. Most months.

Introduced from Europe.

S. *jamesiana*—Sticky Starwort. Fig. 51. Plant somewhat hairy and sticky; stem erect, 1–3.5 dm tall; lvs lanceolate, 5–10 cm long; fls with petals 6–10 mm long. Moist meadows, 4000–8000. MCF, MM. May–July.

S. *crispa*—Chamisso's Starwort. Stem weak, hairless, 1–4 dm long; lvs crisped; fls with minute petals. Moist banks and meadows below 11000. MCF, MM. May–Aug.

Chamisso was an early botanist who named the California Poppy.

S. *longipes* — Long-stalked Starwort. Fig. 52. Stem smooth, erect, 1–2.5 dm tall; lvs lanceolate, 1–2.5 cm long; usually 1 fl on a long stalk. Common, moist places, 4500–11000. MCF, MM. June–Aug.

Key to the Genus *Silene* (Catchfly or Campion)

1a—Fls bright red. S. *californica*.
1b—Fls white, pink, or purplish. See 2.

2a—Sepals divided half of length. S. *aperta*.
2b—Sepals not so deeply divided. See 3.

3a—Petals less than 10 mm long. S *menziesii*.
3b—Petals more than 12 mm long. See 4.

4a—Fls nodding. See 5.
4b—Fls nearly erect. See 6.

5a—Petal tip 2-lobed. S. *bridgesii*.
5b—Petal tip deeply 4-lobed. S. *lemmonii*.

6a—Petal tip with 4-lobes. See 7.
6b—Petal tip with 2-lobes. See 9.

7a—2 outer lobes of 4 on petal smaller. S. *sargentii*.
7b—All 4 petal lobes equal length. See 8.

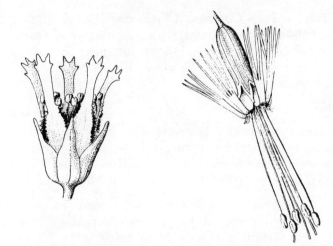

Fig. 53 *Silene aperta*   Fig. 54 *Silene lemmoni*

8a—2 small appendages on center of petal. *S. occidentalis.*
8b—Appendages of petal with ragged edge. *S. montana.*

9a—Sepals hairy and sticky. *S. verecunda.*
9b—Sepals few haired, not sticky. *S. douglasii.*

Most species of *Silene* have many gland-tipped hairs which tend to entrap insects, hence the name catchfly.

Silene californica—California Indian Pink. Pl. 3e. Stem 1.5–4 dm tall; fls bright red. Frequent in semishaded woods below 6000 on w. slope. FW, C, MCF. March–Aug.

The only *Silene* in the Sierra with bright red flowers.

S. aperta—Naked Campion. Fig. 53. Stem 1.5–3.5 dm tall; fls whitish, petal tip with 4 shallow lobes, no appendages on petal. Dry flats under trees, 8000–9000 in Tulare Co. only. MCF. July–Aug.

S. menziesii—Menzies' Campion. Stem 0.5 to 2 dm tall, sticky hairs; fls white, petal tip broadly 2-lobed with small appendages above middle. Woods and near small streams, 6000–11000, widespread. MCF. June–July.

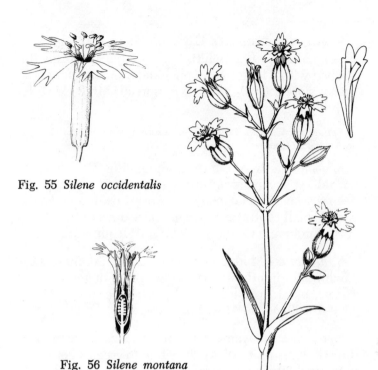

Fig. 55 *Silene occidentalis*

Fig. 56 *Silene montana*

Fig. 57 *Silene verecunda*

Named for Archibald Menzies who was Captain Vancouver's physician and naturalist aboard the exploration ship *Discovery*.

S. *bridgesii*—Bridge's Campion. Stem 3–8 dm tall; fls dirty white, petal tip narrowly 2-lobed with two appendages on middle with ragged edges. Open slopes, 2500–8000 on w. slope. FW, MCF, MM. June–July.

S. *lemmonii*—Lemmon's Campion. Fig. 54. Stem 1.5–4.5 dm tall, sticky hairs; fls yellowish white to pink, petal tip of 4 long narrow lobes and 2 tiny appendages on middle of petal. Open areas, 3500–8000. FW, MCF, MM. June–Aug.

Named for John Lemmon who collected plants along the east side of the Sierra and elsewhere.

S. *sargentii*—Sargent's Campion. Stem 1–1.5 dm tall, sticky hairs; fls few, whitish to rose-purple, petal tip 4-lobed with 2 large center ones and 2 small outer ones. Rocky slopes, 6500–12000, widespread. MCF, MM, S, A. July–Aug.

Named for Charles Sargent who wrote a comprehensive book on American trees.

S. *occidentalis*—Western Campion. Fig. 55. Stem 3–6 dm tall, sticky hairs on upper stem; fls 10–25, flesh to deep rose, each petal long and narrow, petal tip 4-lobed with 2 small central appendages. Dry open areas, 4000–7000, Tuolumne Co. north. MCF, MM. June–July.

S. *montana*—Mountain Campion. Fig. 56. Stem 1.5–4.5 dm tall, slightly sticky; fls few, white tinged pink or purple, petal tip 2-lobed with each lobe also 2-lobed, 4500–10000. MCF, MM. June–Aug.

S. *verecunda*—Cuyamaca Campion. Fig. 57. Stem 1–3 dm tall, hairs quite sticky; fls white to greenish or pink, petal tip 2-lobed and each of central apendages 2-lobed. Dry slopes, 5000–11000, of s. Sierra. MCF, S, A. June–Aug.

S. *douglasii*—Douglas's Campion. (See p. 54.) Stem 1–4 dm tall, each stem few-flowered; fls creamy white, petal tip 2 short lobes. Dry areas, 5000–10000, mostly Donner Pass and north. MCF, S. June–Aug.

Genus *Tunica*

Tunica prolifera—Proliferous Pink. Stems slender, 3–5 dm tall, fls pink, similar to a miniature single-petaled carnation. Common as a pink mass under foothill oaks, Nevada Co. and north below 3000. FW, C. May–early June.

Introduced from Europe, *T. prolifera* is rapidly spreading throughout the foothills.

1a—*Aconitum columbianum.*

1b—*Anemone drummondii.*

1c—*Aquilegia formosa.*

1d—*Caltha howellii.*

1e—*Aquilegia pubescens.*

1f—*Ranunculus muricatus.*

1g—*Ranunculus hystriculus.*

Plate 1

2a—*Paeonia brownii.*

2b—*Limnanthes alba.*

2c—*Eremocarpus setigerus.*

2d—*Arabis glabra.*

2e—*Thalictrum fendleri.*

2f—*Viola glabella.*

2g—*Argemone munita.*

Plate 2

3a—*Arabis perennans.*

3b—*Erysimum perenne.*

3c—*Draba paysonii.*

3d—*Arenaria kingii.*

3e—*Silene californica.*

3f—*Stellaria media.*

3g—*Lewisia rediviva.*

Plate 3

4a—*Rumex acetosella.*

4b—*Eriogonum lobbii.*

4c—*Eriogonum ochrocephalum.*

4d—*Oxyria digyna.*

4e—*Calyptridium umbellatum.*

4f—*Dodecatheon subalpinum.*

Plate 4

5b—*Plantago hookeriana.*

5a—*Primula suffrutescens.*

5c—*Sarcodes sanguinea.*

5d—*Pterospora andromdea.*

5e—*Gentiana newberryi.*

5f—*Gentianopsis simplex.*

5g—*Gentianopsis holopetala.*

Plate 5

6a—*Frasera speciosa.*

6b—*Asclepias speciosa.*

6d—*Asclepias cordifolia.*

6c—*Linanthus bicolor.*

6e—*Linanthus montanus.*

6f—*Polemonium eximum.*

6g—*Linanthus ciliatus.*

Plate 6

7a—*Phlox speciosa.*

7b—*Amsinckia intermedia.*

7c—*Cryptantha nubigena.*

7d—*Collinsia heterophylla.*

7e—*Verbascum thapsus.*

7g—*Mimulus torreyi.*

7f—*Mimulus angustatus.*

7h—*Nemophila maculata.*

Plate 7

8c—*Castilleja chromosa.*

8b—*Penstemon rydbergii.*

8a—*Penstemon davidsonii.*

8d—*Castilleja lemmonii.*

8e—*Castilleja nana.*

8f—*Pedicularis groenlandica.*

8g—*Penstemon speciosus.*

Plate 8

9a—*Marrubium vulgare.*

9b—*Dudleya cymosa.*

9c—*Ivesia lycopodioides.*

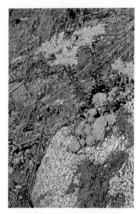

9d—*Sedum spathulifolium.*

9e—*Lupinus densiflorus.*

9f—*Sedum rosea.*

Plate 9

10a—*Lupinus latifolius.*

10b—*Lupinus stiversii.*

10c—*Lathyrus latifolius.*

10d—*Lotus oblongifolius.*

10e—*Astragalus whitneyi.*

10f—*Clarkia biloba.*

Plate 10

11a—*Asarum hartwegii.*

11b—*Spenosciadium capitellatum.*

11c—*Cymopterus cinearius.*

11d—*Perideridia parishii.*

11e—*Haplopappus acaulis.*

11f—*Wyethia mollis.*

11g—*Wyethia bolanderi.*

Plate 11

12b—*Helianthella
californica.*

12a—*Balsamorhiza
deltoidea.*

12c—*Aster alpigenus.*

12d—*Eriophyllum lanatum.*

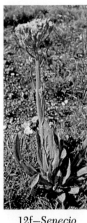

12e—*Helenium
hoopesii.*

12f—*Senecio
integerrimus.*

12g—*Helenium
bigelovii.*

Plate 12

13a—*Hulsea algida.*

13b—*Erigeron pygmaeus.*

13c—*Arnica mollis.*

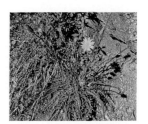

13d—*Agoseris retrorsa.*

13e—*Centaurea solstitialis.*

13f—*Antennaria rosea.*

13g—*Tragopogon porrifolius.*

Plate 13

14a—*Calochortus albus.*

14b—*Calochortus leichtlinii.*

14c—*Zigadenus venenosus.*

14d—*Xerophyllum tenax.*

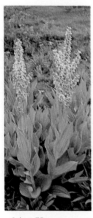

14e—*Veratrum californicum.*

14f—*Fritillaria atropurpurea.*

14g—*Camassia leichtlinii.*

Plate 14

15a—*Smilacina stellata.*

15b—*Lilium humboldtii.*

15c—*Lilium parvum.*

15d—*Lilium pardalinum.*

15e—*Allium amplectens.*

15f—*Triteleia laxa.*

Plate 15

16a—*Triteleia scabra.*   16b—*Brodiaea elegans.*

16c—*Iris missouriensis.*

16d—*Epipactis gigantea.*

16e—*Spiranthes porrifolia.*   16f—*Habenaria dilatata.*

Plate 16

Fig. 58 *Calandrinia ciliata*

KEY TO THE FAMILY PORTULACACEAE
(PURSLANE)

1a—Sepals 2, stamens 5 or fewer. See 2.
1b—Sepals 2–8, stamens more than 5 (except *L. tri-phylla*). See 8.

2a—Style 3-branched. See 3.
2b—Style unbranched. *Calyptridum umbellatum.*

3a—Fls dark red. *Calandrinia ciliata.*
3b—Fls white to pink. See 4.

4a—Plant from slender rootstock. See 5 (*Montia*).
4b—Plant from roundish bulb. See 7 (*Claytonia*).

5a—Lvs large fleshy, rounded. *M. perfoliata.*
5b—Lvs linear to oblong. See 6.

6a—Petals 5–8 mm long. *M. chamissoi.*
6b—Petals 3 mm long. *M. funstonii.*

7a—Basal lvs on long petiole. *Claytonia nevadensis.*
7b—Basal lvs oblanceolate, short petioled. *C. lanceol-ata.*

[65]

8a—Plants without basal lvs, small round bulb. *Lewisia triphylla.*
8b—Plants with several to many basal lvs. See 9.

9a—Stems 1–3 dm tall, fls high above basal lvs. See 10.
9b—Stems 1 dm or less, fls close to lvs. See 11.

10a—Lf blade entire. *L. congdonii.*
10b—Lf blade toothed. *L. cantelowii.*

11a—Sepals greenish. See 12.
11b—Sepals pinkish similar to petals. *L. rediviva.*

12a—Sepals toothed and veined. *L. pygmaea.*
12b—Sepals not toothed or veined. See 13.

13a—Fls white. *L. nevadensis.*
13b—Fls pink. *L. sierrae.*

Genus *Calandrinia*

Calandrinia ciliata var. *menziesii*—Red Maids. Fig. 58. Stem fleshy, 1–4 dm tall; fl with 5 red petals. Early spring plant, moist semishade below 6000, very common in disturbed places. FW, MCF, MM, SS. Feb.–May.

Seeds provide food for 16 different bird species.

Genus *Montia* (Indian Lettuce)

Montia perfoliata—Miner's Lettuce. Fig. 59. Lvs large, fleshy, green, often surrounding stem, so that the pink to white fls appear to emerge from the round lvs. Moist shaded places, common below 6000. FW, C, MCF. Feb.–June.

Leaves and stems may be eaten raw or boiled. The roots are also edible. Early-day California miners ate *M. perfoliata*, and it is now grown in Europe as a vegetable.

M. chamissoi—Toad Lily. Stems creeping or floating; with erect branches, 5–15 cm tall; lvs opposite; flvs 3–8, pink or white, 5–8 mm long. Wet places, 4000–11000. MCF, S, MM. June–Aug.

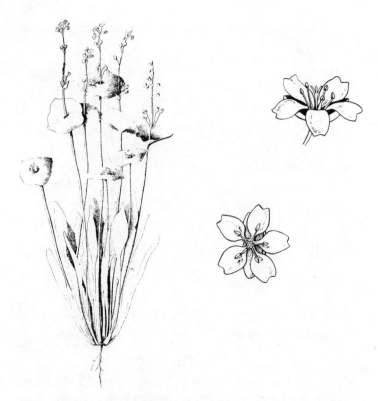

Fig. 59 *Montia perfoliata*

Genus *Claytonia* (Springbeauty)

The small bulbs may be eaten raw or cooked, and they are good when added to stews or salads.

Claytonia nevadensis — Sierra Nevada Springbeauty. From fleshy roots; lvs basal on long petioles 5–10 cm; 2–6 fls, white to pink. Wet places, 8000–12000. MCF. July–Aug.

C. lanceolata — Lance-leaved Springbeauty. From small round bulbs; lvs 1–2, basal, lanceolate; few to 15 fls, pink. Moist shady woods, 4500–8500, Tuolumne Co. north. MCF. May–July.

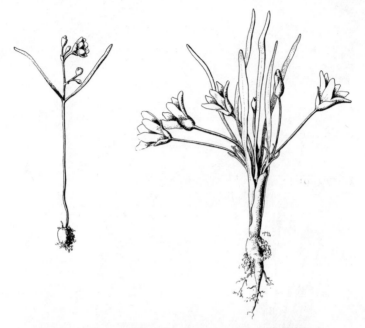

Fig. 60 *Lewisia triphylla*   Fig. 61 *Lewisia nevadensis*

Genus *Calyptridium*

Calyptridium umbellatum — Pussy Paws. Pl. 4e. Plant low, spreading; lvs in dense basal cluster, fls in dense umbel-like mass, rose pink to white, tending to be more white at higher elevations. Open dry rocky places, frequent 2500–13000. FW, MCF, S, A. May–Aug.

Genus *Lewisia* (Lewis's Flower)

This genus is named for Captain Meriwether Lewis of the Lewis and Clark expedition. He observed that the Indians of the Northwest ate plants in this genus prepared in various ways. The taste can be very bitter unless you know how to cook it.

Lewisia triphylla—Three-leaved Lewisia. Fig. 60. From small round bulb; stem slender, with no basal lvs, 3–10 cm tall with 3 linear lvs just below white or pink fls. Damp sandy meadows, 4500–11000. MCF, S. June–Aug.

L. congdonii—Columbia Lewisia. Lvs many, lanceolate, in basal cluster, 5–10 cm long; stem finely branched, flowering, 2–4 dm tall; fls rose. Often on rocky cliffs, 6000–9000, Mariposa Co. and south. MCF. May–June.

L. cantelowii — Cantelow's Lewisia. Similar to *L. congdonii*, except basal lf blade edges toothed. Similar habitat, Nevada Co. and north. FW, MCF. May–June.

L. rediviva—Bitterroot. Pl. 3g. Plant is low cluster of round linear lvs, 2–5 cm long; fls very large, showy, rose to light pink. Open semibare places, 10000 and lower on both sides of the Sierra. FW, MCF, S, PJ. March–June.

State flower of Montana.

L. pygmaea—Pygmy Lewisia. Plant is low cluster of narrow linear lvs 3–8 cm long; stems flowering, mixed in with lvs; fls white to pink, sepal rounded and toothed along margin. Damp sand or gravel throughout A. July–Sept.

L. nevadensis—Nevada Lewisia. Fig. 61. Similar to *L. pygmaea* but sepals broadly ovate and margins not toothed. Wet meadows, 4500–12000. MCF, MM, S, A. May–July.

L. sierrae—Sierra Lewisia. Plant small, tufted, 1–2.5 cm tall; fls pink, 4–5 mm long. Moist places, 9000–14000, Tuolumne Meadows and south. MM, S, A. July–Aug.

1 millimeter
10 millimeters = 1 centimeter = 13/32 inch
10 centimeters = 1 decimeter = ca. 4 inches
10 decimeters = 1 meter = 3.3 feet

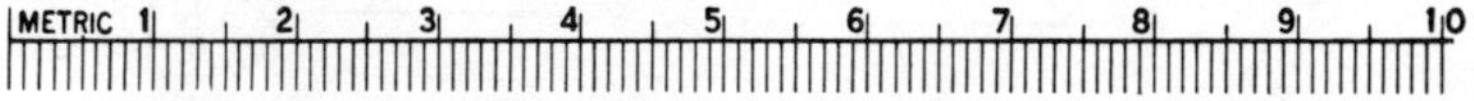

Fig. 62 Metric scale 1:1

KEY TO THE FAMILY POLYGONACEAE
(BUCKWHEAT)

1a—Lvs without brown papery sheath at base. *Eriogonum*.

1b—Lvs with definite brown papery sheath at base. See 2.

2a—Fls 4- or 6-parted. See 3.

2b—Fls 5-parted. *Polygonum*.

3a—Lvs kidney-shaped, fls 4-parted. *Oxyria digyna*.

3b—Lvs variously elongated, fls 6-parted. *Rumex*.

Seeds of many species in the buckwheat family were used by the Indians to make flour. A large variety of birds, small mammals and deer depend on the seeds for food. The Mormon Metal-Mark, Hair Streak, Copper, and Blue butterflies use this family extensively for food.

Key to the Genus *Eriogonum* (Wild Buckwheat)

1a—Individual fls with narrow enlongated base, 2 to several leafy bracts below fls. See 2.

1b—Individual fls with rounded base, 3 small bracts below fls, not leafy. See 6.

2a—Invols with lobes half as long as fl and reflexed. See 3.

2b—Invols with lobes shorter than tube, sub-erect. toothlike. See 4.

3a—Fl stems nearly upright. *E. umbellatum*.

3b—Fl stems flat on ground. *E. lobbii*.

4a—Outside of fl hairy. *E. latens*.

4b—Outside of fl not hairy. See 5.

5a—Lvs densely white-hairy on both surfaces. *E. incanum*.

5b—Top of lf without hair, greenish. *E. marifolium*.

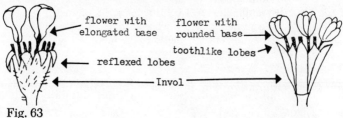

flower with elongated base

flower with rounded base

toothlike lobes

reflexed lobes

Invol

Fig. 63

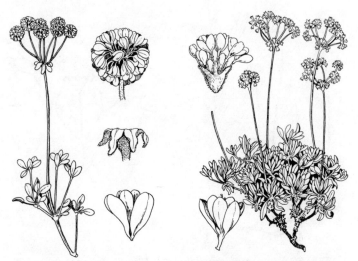

Fig. 64 *Eriogonum umbellatum*   Fig. 65 *Eriogonum incanum*

6a—Invols not ribbed. See 7.
6b—Invols 5–6-ribbed (veined). See 8.

7a—Lvs linear. *E. spergulinum*.
7b—Lvs ovate, stem inflated. *E. inflatum*.

8a—Flowering stem divided with fls on each. See 9.
8b—Flowering stem a single head of fls. See 10.

9a—Lvs more than 2 cm long. *E. nudum*.
9b—Lvs less than 2 cm long. *E. wrightii*.

10a—Alternate petals of a fl twice as large. *E. ovalifolium*.
10b—All petals same size and shape. *E. ochrocephalum*.

Eriogonum umbellatum—Sulphur-flowered Eriogonum.
Fig. 64. Plant large, cushionlike, 2–6 dm tall; lvs spoon-like; fls yellow turning reddish with age. Very common in open rocky places, 2500–10000. FW, MCF, MM, S, A, PJ. May–Aug.

Indians made a tea from the roots for colds.

E. lobbii—Lobb's Eriogonum. Pl. 4*b*. Lvs and stem spread flat on open rocky ledges; fls pinkish. 5500–12000, widespread. S, A. June–Aug.

E. latens—Onion-flowered Eriogonum. Lvs in basal

[71]

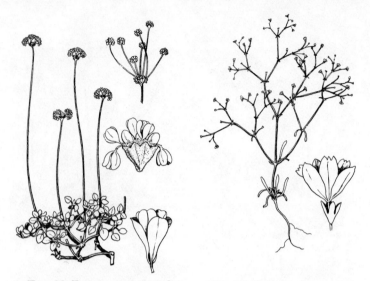

Fig. 66 *Eriogonum marifolium*   Fig. 67 *Eriogonum spergulinum*

cluster, rounded blade on long petioles; fl stem long, leafless, with large ball of cream to pale yellow fls, stem and ball of fls similar to flowering habit of onions. Dry slopes, 6500–11000, s. Sierra. A. July–Aug.

E. incanum—Frosty Eriogonum. Fig. 65. Plants are cushiony mats, 1–2 dm across; lvs and stems with dense white hairs; fls in headlike clusters, pale yellow without hairs. Open rocky slopes, 7000–12000, main crest. S, A. July–Sept.

E. marifolium—Marum-leaved Eriogonum. Fig. 66. Stem loosely branched, forming mats with tufts of lvs here and there; lvs ovate, densely white hairy underneath, hairless and green on upper side; fls yellowish, often with red lines. Dry sandy flats, 3500–11000, Fresno Co. and north. MCF, MM. July–Aug.

E. spergulinum—Spurry Eriogonum. Fig. 67. Plant small, delicate, with many fine branches, 1–5 cm tall; lvs linear on all parts of stem; fls white with rose lines. Flats and gentle slopes, 5000–12000, widespread. MCF, MM, S. June–Aug.

[72]

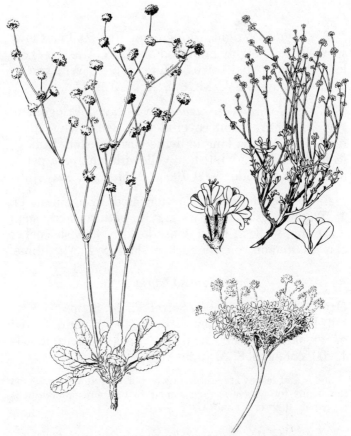

Fig. 68 *Eriogonum nudum* Fig. 69 *Eriogonum wrightii* Fig. 70 *ovalifolium*

E. inflatum—Desert Trumpet. Lvs all basal; stem leafless and much branched, 2–10 dm tall, conspicuously inflated at top of each joint; fls yellow with some red brown. Below 9000 along e. slope. PJ, SS. July–Aug.

Indians used the inflated stem as a pipe to smoke the local wild tobacco.

E. nudum—Naked-stemmed Eriogonum. Fig. 68. Lvs basal, 2–6 cm long, white underneath, dark green above; stems without lvs; fls white to occasionally pink. Most common species below 8000 on w. slope. FW, MCF, MM, S. June–Nov.

[73]

E. wrightii—Wright's Eriogonum. Fig. 69. Plant low; stems leafless, highly branched; lvs lanceolate, 1.5–3 cm long; fls elongated spikes, white to pink. Widespread at all elevations. FW, MCF, S, A, PJ. Aug–Oct.

E. ovalifolium var. *nivale*—Oval-leaved Eriogonum. Fig. 70. Entire plant covered with dense white hair; lvs oval, 5–15 mm long in dense cushion; stem leafless; fls in dense head, whitish to yellowish, alternate petals of fl twice as wide. 5000–10000. MM, S, A. May–July.

E. ochrocephalum—Ocher-flowered Eriogonum. Pl. 4*c*. Plant is cushionlike; lvs grayish both surfaces; stem flowering, leafless; fls in dense head, yellowish (ocher clay). Often on volcanic rock, e. slope. S, A. May–June.

Genus *Oxyria*

Oxyria digyna—Mountain Sorrel. Pl. 4*d*. Stems 6–25 cm tall; lvs rounded, kidney-shaped, 1–3 cm wide; fls red or greenish, loosely arranged. Rocky places, 8000–13000, common. S, A. June–Aug.

Stems and leaves are edible raw or boiled. Indians fermented the plants for winter storage similar to the way sauerkraut is prepared. Rich in vitamin C.

Key to the Genus *Polygonum* (Knotweed)

1a—Fls in terminal spikes with no leafy bracts present. See 2.
1b—Fls in side branches, or spike with leafy bracts. See 4.

2a—Dry slopes, spike few-flowered. *P. davisiae*.
2b—Wet places, spike densely flowered. See 3.

3a—Lvs oblong, fls pink or white. *P. bistortoides*.
3b—Lvs lance-ovate, fls rose. *P. coccineum*.

4a—Stems round. *P. aviculare*.
4b—Stems strongly angled. See 5.

5a—Lvs ovate. *P. minimum*.
5b—Lvs linear-lance oblong. See 6.

6a—Lvs 1–4 cm long, fls reddish. *P. douglasii*.
6b—Lvs less than 1 cm long, fls greensh. *P. kelloggii*.

Fig. 71 *Polygonum bistortoides*

Polygonum davisiae—Davis's Knotweed. Stem 1–4 dm tall; lvs many, ovate, without petioles; fls whitish to purplish green, ovary with 3 short separate styles. Rocky places, 5000–9000, Dardanelles, Tuolumne Co., and north. MM, S, A. June–Sept.

P. bistortoides—Western Bistort or Snakeweed. Fig. 71. Rootstock thick; stem 2–7 dm tall; lvs oblong mostly near base of stem; fls pink or white in dense terminal mass, style 3-lobed. Soggy meadows, 5000–10000. MM. June–Aug.

The roots may be used as a starch source when roasted, but they are bitter if undercooked.

P. coccineum—Water Smartweed. Stem near ground; lvs lance oblong, 5–10 cm long; fls rose in dense terminal masses, ovary round, style 2-lobed. Highly variable plant found on dry land and in ponds below 10000. SL. June–Aug.

P. aviculare—Common Knotweed. Stems sprawling; lvs many, lanceolate, 5–20 mm long, bluish green; fls greenish with pinkish margins, ovary without apparent style. Common in disturbed places, most communities. All year.

Indians used the seeds to make flour.

P. minimum—Leafy Dwarf Knotweed. Annual. Plant scruffy, 5–15 cm tall; lvs many, ovate, 5–15 mm long; fls greenish-white, stamens 3–5. Damp open meadows, 5000–12000, widespread. MCF, MM. July–Sept.

P. douglasii—Douglas's Knotweed. (See p. 54.) Stem slender, 1–4 dm tall; lvs lanceolate 1–4 cm long, pale green; 1–3 fls drooping, reddish, ovary elongate. Dry areas in meadows 4000–9000. Widespread. MM. June–Sept.

P. kelloggii—Kellogg's Knotweed. Stems tufted, 3–8 cm tall; lvs linear, 0.5–1 cm long; fls green with white margins, stamens 3. Damp places, 4500–12000, widespread. MM, S. June–Sept.

Named for Albert Kellogg, one of the founders of the California Academy of Sciences.

Key to the Genus *Rumex* (Dock or Wild Rhubarb)

1a—Fls with both anthers and pistils, acid to taste. See 2.
1b—Fls unisexual, not acid to taste. See 3.

2a—Lvs arrowhead-shaped. *R. acetosella.*
2b—Lvs narrowing at base. *R. paucifolius.*

3a—Stem without basal lvs, often lying down. *R. salicifolius.*
3b—Stem with basal lvs, erect. *R. crispus.*

Stems and leaves may be eaten like rhubarb, but the acid concentration can be poisonous if too much is consumed at one time. Deformed reddish seeds are due to the Dock Seed Midge.

Rumex acetosella—Sheep Sorrel. Pl. 4a. Stem 1–4 dm

tall; lvs arrowhead-shaped, 2–6 cm long; fls yellowish in terminal panicles, turning reddish in age. Common all communities. All year.

Introduced from Europe.

R. paucifolius subsp. *gracilescens*—Few-leaved Dock. Stem 1.5–7 dm tall; lvs long, narrow, 4–10 cm long; fls and seeds reddish. Damp places, mostly 10000–13000, Mt. Whitney to Sonora Pass. MCF, MM, S, A. July–Sept.

R. salicifolius—Willow-leaved Dock. Stem 3–9 dm tall; lvs to 13 cm long; fls and seeds in thick mass, seed large, with very narrow papery wings. Common below 7000, many communities. All year.

R. crispus—Curly-leaved Dock. Stem 5–12 dm tall; lvs lanceolate, 1–3 dm long, margins curly; seed small, surrounded by wide papery margin. Common in disturbed places, old barns, at low elevations. FW, C, MCF, SS. March–July.

Introduced from Europe.

KEY TO THE FAMILY PRIMULACEAE
(PRIMROSE)

1a—All lvs basal, fls on leafless stem. See 2.
1b—Stems leafy, fls on leafy stems. See 7.

2a—Petals folded backward. See 3. (*Dodecatheon*).
2b—Petals spreading, bright red. *Primula*.

3a—Petals 4. See 4.
3b—Petals 5. See 5.

4a—Lvs hairless, roots with tiny bulblets. *D. alpinum*.
4b—Lvs hairy, roots without bulblets. *D. jeffreyi*.

5a—Plants hairless, roots with tiny bulblets. See 6.
5b—Plants very hairy, roots without bulblets. *D. Redolens.*

[77]

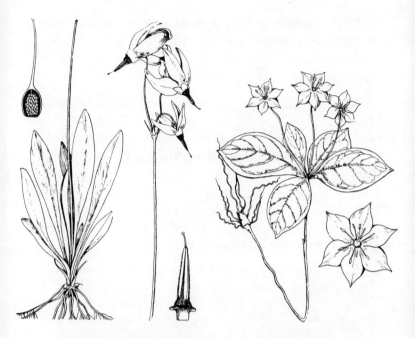

Fig. 72 *Dodecatheon alpinum*   Fig. 73 *Trientalis latifolia*

6a—Lower foothills of Sierra, roots white. *D. Hansenii.*
6b—Above 7000, roots reddish. *D. subalpinum.*

7a—Lvs at top of stem, umbrellalike. *Trientalis.*
7b—Many lvs on sprawlng stem, fls orange-red. *Anagallis.*

Genus *Dodecatheon* (Shooting Stars)

The stems and leaves are reported to be edible after boiling or roasting.

Dodecatheon alpinum—Alpine Shooting Star. Fig. 72. Plant hairless; stem 0.5–1.5 dm tall; fl corolla tube base maroon, yellow above, petals magenta-lavender. Wet places, 4000–12000. MM. June–Aug.

D. jeffreyi—Jeffrey's Shooting Star. Stem 1.5–6 dm tall; fl corolla tube base maroon, yellow above, petals magenta-lavender. Wet places, below 10000, most common Shooting Star. MM, S, A. June–Aug.

Named for John Jeffrey, who was sent to California in 1850 by a group of Scottish horticulturalists to collect seeds. He discovered this species as well as the Jeffrey Pine of the eastern Sierra.

D. redolens—Mountaineer Shooting Star. Stem 3–6 dm tall; lvs with strong odor, hairless; fl with 5 petal lobes magenta to lavender. Damp places, 8000–12000, southern Sierra. MCF, MM, S, A. July–Aug.

D. hansenii—Hansen's Shooting Star. Stem 1–2.5 dm tall; fl corolla tube maroon with yellow band; roots white with tiny bulblets. Lower western foothills. FW, C, PP. April–May.

D. subalpinum—Sierra Shooting Star. Pl. 4f. Stem 0.5–1.5 dm tall; fl corolla tube maroon with yellow band, 5 petal lobes magenta to white. Moist places, 7000–13000, Yosemite and south. MCF, MM. May–July.

Genus *Primula*

Primula suffrutescens—Sierra Primrose. Pl. 5a. Plant with tufted base of lvs; stem flowering, 4–10 cm tall; fls bright red with yellow throat. Slightly shaded places about cliff bases, above 8000. A. July–Aug.

Flowers shortly after snow melts.

Genus *Trientalis*

Trientalis latifolia—Star Flower. Fig. 73. Stem bare, 0.5–2 dm tall, with 4–6 lvs in umbrellalike whorl at top, fls pink. Very common, shaded woods, below 6000. MCF. April–July.

Genus *Anagallis*

Anagallis arvensis—Scarlet Pimpernel. Fig. 74. Plant low, spreading, much branched; lvs ovate; fls with pet-

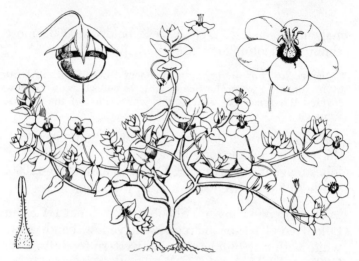

Fig. 74 *Anagallis arvensis*

als joined into very shallow bowl, scarlet to orange. Common in disturbed places at low elevations. FW, C, MCF. Flowers most of year.

Introduced from Europe.

FAMILY PLANTAGINACEAE (PLANTAIN)

Key to the Genus *Plantago*

1a—Lvs gray-green. *Plantago hookeriana.*
1b—Lvs green. See 2.

2a—Lvs broadly ovate. *P. major.*
2b—Lvs lanceolate. *P. lanceolata.*

Plantago hookeriana var. *californica*—Hooker's California Plantain. Pl 5b. Fig. 75. Plant low growing, 5–20 cm tall; lvs linear, gray-green, near base; fls a dense cluster, brownish, on stalk. Very common in all grassy areas at lower elevations. FW, C, PJ. March–June.

P. major—Common Plantain. Fig. 76. Lvs broadly ovate, in basal cluster; fls many, tiny, brownish, in spikes on leafless stem, 0.5–5 dm tall. Damp places,

Fig. 75 *Plantago hookeriana*   Fig. 76 *Plantago major*

common, often found near leaking faucets. FW, MCF, SS. Most of the year.

Introduced from Europe.

P. lanceolata—English Plantain or Buckhorn. Lvs. lanceolate in basal clusters; fl spike similar to *P. major*. Common in dry places such as driveways. FW, MCF, SS. All year.

Introduced from Europe.

KEY TO THE FAMILY PYROLACEAE
(WINTERGREEN)

1a—Lvs green. See 2.
1b—Lvs not green, stem fleshy. See 7.

2a—Fls in racemes. See 3. (*Pyrola*).
2b—Fls in a corymb (flat topped raceme). See 6.

3a—Style strongly bent near base, collar on stigma. See
    See 4.
3b—Style straight, no stigma collar. See 5.

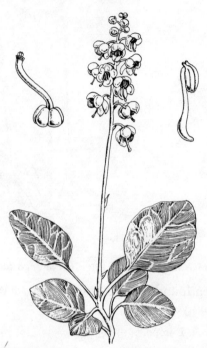

Fig. 77 *Pyrola picta*

4a—Petals red to purplish. *P. californica.*
4b—Petals greenish to whitish. *P. picta.*

5a—Fls in spiral, white to pink. *P. minor.*
5b—Fls all on one side, yellow-green. *P. secunda.*

6a—One to 3 white fls. *Chimaphila menziesii.*
6b—Three to 7 pink fls. *C. umbellata.*

7a—Stems striped red and white. *Allotropa.*
7b—Stems not striped. See 8.

8a—Stem and fls bright red. *Sarcodes.*
8b—Stem and fls brownish. *Peterospora.*

Genus *Pyrola*

Pyrola californica—Bog Wintergreen. Lvs oval, 3–8 cm long, shiny green, in basal clusters; fls red to purple on stalk 2–4 dm tall. Shady woods, 4000–9000. MCF. July–Sept.

P. *picta*—White-veined Wintergreen. Fig. 77. Lvs elliptic with white veins; fls greenish to whitish on stalk 1–2 cm tall. Shady woods below 7500. MCF. June–Aug.

P. *minor*—Common Wintergreen. Lvs roundish, dull green, in basal clusters; fls white to pink on stalk 6–15 cm tall. Occasional in wet shady places, 7000–10000. MCF. June–Aug.

P. *secunda*—One-sided Wintergreen. Lvs ovate in basal cluster, shining green; fls yellow to green, all on one side of stalk. Dry shady woods, 3000–11000. MCF. July–Sept.

Genus *Chimaphila*

Chimaphila menziesii—Little Prince's Pine. Lvs lance-oblong along stem, 1–1.5 dm tall; fls white. Shady woods, 2500–8000, common. MCF. June–Aug.

C. *umbellata* var. *occidentalis*—Western Prince's Pine. Lvs in whorls of 3–8, oblanceolate with saw-toothed edges; fls pink. Dry shady woods below 10000. MCF. June–Aug.

Indians mixed Western Prince's Pine with tobacco to smoke. A tasty drink can be made by boiling the leaves and stems and allowing the liquid to cool. It is used in the manufacture of root beer and in some medicines.

Genus *Allotropa*

Allotropa virgata—Sugar Stick. Stems striped red and white like a candy-cane, 1–5 dm tall. Dark shady woods, below 10000. MCF. July–Aug.

Sugar Stick is a special find! The plant lives on decaying humas as a saphrophyte, and thus obtains its nutrients without photosynthesis.

Genus *Sarcodes*

Sarcodes sanguinea—Snow Plant. Pl 5c. Fls and stem a bright red, 1.5–3 dm tall. Shady woods, 4000–8000. MCF. May–Aug.

Shortly after the snow melts the flowers appear. It lives on decaying humus, as does the Sugar Stick. It is protected by law, so do not pick!

Genus *Pterospora*

Pterospora andromedea—Pine Drops. Pl. 5d. Stems brownish, 4–10 dm tall, common in shady woods below 8500. MCF. July–Aug.

A saprophyte, like the Snow Plant.

KEY TO THE FAMILY GENTIANACEAE (GENTIAN)

1a—Fls long tubular. See 2.
1b—Fls open bowl-like. See 5.

2a—Fls white with greenish spots. *Gentiana newberryi*.
2b—Fls blue to purple. See 3.

3a—Fls 7–20 mm long. *G. amarella*.
3b—Fls 25–50 mm long. See 4.

4a—Petal lobes equal to tube length. *Gentianopsis simplex*.
4b—Petal lobes half the length of tube. *G. holopetala*.

---

1 millimeter
10 millimeters = 1 centimeter = 13/32 inch
10 centimeters = 1 decimeter = ca. 4 inches
10 decimeters = 1 meter = 3.3 feet

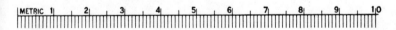

Fig. 78 Metric scale 1:1

Fig. 79 *Gentiana amarella*   Fig. 80 *Centaurium venustum*

5a—Fls pink. *Centaurium venustum.*
5b—Fls greenish. See 6.

6a—Petals 5. *Swertia perennis.*
6b—Petals 4. See 7.

7a—Stem 1–2 m tall. *Frasera speciosa.*
7b—Stem 1–7 dm tall. See 8.

8a—Stem lvs whorled. *F. tubulosa.*
8b—Stem lvs opposite. See 9.

9a—Fls in narrow spike, w. Sierra. *F. albicaulis.*
9b—Fls in open panicle, e. Sierra. *F. puberulenta*

Genus *Gentiana*

Gentiana newberryi—Alpine Gentian. Pl. 5*e*. Stems sprawling, 4–12 cm tall; fls white with greenish spots,

[85]

2–3 cm long. Wet meadows, 7000–12000, common. MM, S, A. July–Sept.

Named for John Newberry, botanist and physician on the Pacific Railway Surveys of the 1850s.

G. amarella—Felwort. Fig. 79. Stems slender, 0.5–5 dm tall; fls lavender, tubular 8–20 mm long. Wet meadows, 4500–11000. MM. June–Sept.

Genus *Gentianopsis*

Gentianopsis simplex—Hiker's Gentian. Pl. 5*f*. Stem 0.5–2 dm tall; fl single, blue, 2.5–4 cm long, 4-lobed, lobes same length as corolla tube. Wet meadows, 4000–9500. MM. July–Sept.

G. holopetala—Sierra Gentian. Pl. 5*g*. Stem 0.5–4 dm tall; fls blue-purple, 4-lobed, 3–5 cm long. Common in meadows, 6000–11000, Tuolomne Co. and south. MM, S, A. July–Sept.

Genus *Centaurium*

Centaurium venustum subsp. *abramsii*—Canchalagua or Beautiful Centaury. Fig. 80. Plant simply branched, 1–3 dm tall with ovate lvs; fls dark pink with a white throat. Common in grassy places in early summer along w. slope below 5000. FW, MCF. May–Aug.

Genus *Swertia*

Swertia perennis—Perennial Swertia. Stem 1–3 dm tall, fls greenish-white with bluish-purple tint. Wet meadows, 8000–10500. MM, S, A. July–Sept.

Genus *Frasera*

Frasera speciosa—Giant Frasera. Pl. 6*a*. Stem 1–2 m tall; fls greenish-white, dotted with purple. Dry open places, 6500–10000. MM. July–Aug.

Indians ate the fleshy root raw, roasted, or boiled and often mixed it with salad greens.

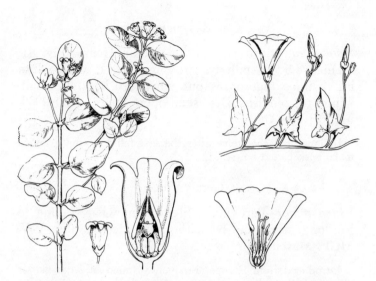

Fig. 81 *Apocynum androsaemifolium*   Fig. 82 *Convolvulus arvensis*

F. tubulosa—Kern Frasera. Stems solitary, 2–7 dm tall; lvs opposite, white margined, mostly basal; fls white with bluish veins. Dry open places, 6000–9000, Kern River drainage. MCF. May–July.

F. albicaulis—White-stemmed Frasera. Stem with minute white hairs, 2.5–4.5 dm tall; fls greenish-white with bluish cast. Semi-shade, 4000–6000, w. slope from Nevada Co. North. FW, C. May–July.

F. puberulenta—Inyo Frasera. Stems stout, 1–3 dm tall; lvs minutely hairy, margins white; fls greenish-white with purple dots. Dry open slopes, 8000–11000, on e. slope. MCF, PJ. June–Aug.

KEY TO THE FAMILY APOCYNACEAE
(DOGBANE)

1a—Fls small, white to pinkish. *Apocynum.*
1b—Fls large, blue. *Vinca.*

[87]

Genus *Apocynum*

Apocynum androsaemifolium—Indian Hemp. Fig. 81.
Stem 2–4.5 dm tall; lvs drooping, ovate, with white
milky juice that oozes out when crushed; fls small,
white to pinkish. Dry semi-open areas, 4000–9000.
MCF. June–Aug.

Indians used the stems after the first fall frost for string to
make baskets and bowstrings.

Genus *Vinca*

Vinca major—Periwinkle. Stems somewhat trailing to
1 m long; stems and lvs with milky juice; fls blue. FW,
MCF. March–Sept.

Introduced from Europe. Frequently found in large masses
about old mining homesteads. Sometimes used as a ground cover.

KEY TO THE FAMILY ASCLEPIADACEAE (MILKWEED)

1a—Lvs densely white wooly. See 2.
1b—Lvs hairless or nearly so. See 3.

2a—Fls purplish to dark maroon. *Asclepias californica*.
2b—Fls light rose, aging yellowish. *A. speciosa*.

3a—Fls dark red-purple. *A. cordifolia*.
3b—Fls greenish-white. *A. fascicularis*

Indians used the milkweeds in many ways: The stems were a
source of string; the juice served as a remedy for rattlesnake bite
or for treating sores on horses; the stems; leaves, and flowers
were eaten after processing. Monarch Butterfly caterpillars—the
large, green-and-yellow striped ones—are dependent on the genus
Asclepias for a food source.

Genus *Asclepias*

Asclepias californica—Round-hooded Milkweed. Stem
1.5–5 dm tall; lvs soft white wooly, milky juice; fls purple to dark moroon in umbels. Dry open slopes, below

6000, Mariposa Co. south. FW, C. April–July.

A. speciosa—Showy Milkweed. Pl. 6*b*. Stems stout in clumps, 5–12 dm tall, soft white hairy, milky juice; fls light rose aging yellowish. Dry open places below 6000 on both slopes of the Sierra. FW, C, MCF. June–July.

The Monarch Butterfly caterpillar is frequently seen on this species.

A. cordifolia—Purple Milkweed. Pl. 6*d*. Stem 3–8 dm tall; lvs and stem hairless and tinted purple, milky juice; fls dark red-purple. Dry semi-open areas below 7000 on w. slope. FW, C. May–July.

A. fascicularis—Narrow-leaf Milkweed. Stems in large clumps, 5–9 dm tall; fls small greenish-white. Often as colonies in dry open areas below 7000 on w. slope. FW, C, MCF. June–Sept.

KEY TO THE FAMILY CONVOLVULACEAE (MORNING GLORY)

1a—Lvs white hairy. See 2.
1b—Lvs green, hairless. See 3.

2a—Dense spreading hair, bracts below sepals ovate. *Calystegia malacophyllus.*
2b—Hair very short, bracts below sepals linear. *C. tomentellus.*

3a—Bracts below sepals arrowheadlike. *C. fulcratus.*
3b—Bracts below sepals linear. *Convolvulus arvensis.*

Genus *Calystegia*

Calystegia tomentellus—Kern Morning Glory. Stem short, trailing; lvs grayish-green with minute hairs; bracts linear immediately below fls. Dry slopes, 4000–6500, Kern Co. FW, MCF. May–July.

C. malacophyllus—Sierra Morning Glory. Stems trailing; lvs with dense white spreading hairs; bracts immediately below fls ovate. Dry slopes below 7500, common. FW, C, MCF. May–Aug.

C. fulcratus—Sonora Morning Glory. Stems long, twining; lvs arrowhead-shaped; bracts below fls are similar to lvs. Dry areas below 8500. FW, C, MCF. May–Aug.

Genus *Convolvulus*

Convolvulus arvensis—Field Bindweed. Fig. 82. Stems long, twining over other plants; lvs arrowhead-shaped; bracts below fls linear. Widespread. FW, C, MCF. May–Oct.

Introduced from Europe.

KEY TO THE FAMILY POLEMONIACEAE (PHLOX)

1a—Calyx bursting as seed capsule matures (look at oldest fl on plant). See 3.
1b—Calyx growing with capsule, not bursting it. See 2.

2a—Lvs pinnately compound. *Polemonium.*
2b—Lvs linear. *Collomia.*

3a—Lvs opposite. See 4.
3b—Lvs alternate. See 5.

4a—Lf edges entire. *Phlox.*
4b—Lfs cleft, fingerlike. *Linanthus.*

5a—Lvs without spiny tips. See 6.
5b—Lvs with spiny tips. *Navarretia.*

6a—Upper stem lvs much smaller. *Gilia.*
6b—Upper stem lvs well developed. See 7.

7a—Lvs with horny tips. *Ipomopsis.*
7b—Lvs without horny tips. *Allophyllum.*

Key to the Genus *Polemonium* (Jacob's Ladder)

1a—Fls in a dense cymose head. *P. eximium.*
1b—Fls in a loose cyme. See 2.

2a—Stems single and erect. *P. caeruleum.*
2b—Stems clustered. See 3.

3a—Below timberline. *P. californicum.*
3b—Above timberline. *P. pulcherrimum.*

*Polemonium eximium—*Sierra Pilot, or Sky Pilot. Pl. 6*f.*
Lvs in basal tuft; fl stem 1–3 dm; fls blue, in a dense
headlike cyme. Dry rocky ridge crests, 10000–14000.
A. June–Aug.

To find this plant you must truly climb in the alpine zone of
the Sierra. At these high altitudes the sky becomes a dark purple
much like the color of Sierra Pilot.

P. caeruleum subsp. *amygdalinum—*Great Polemoni-
um. Stem single, erect, 2–9 dm tall; lvs pinnate; fls blue.
Wet places below 11000, widespread. MCF, S. June–
Aug.

*P. californicum—*Low Polemonium. Stem 1–2 dm tall;
fls in a loose cyme, fl lobes blue with a white corolla
tube. Moist shady places, 6000–10000, w. slope. MCF,
S. June–Aug.

*P. pulcherrimum—*Showy Polemonium. Stem 0.5 to
3 cm tall; fls blue with a yellow corolla tube. Dry open
slopes especially on volcanic rock, 8000–11000. MCF, S.
June–Aug.

Key to the Genus *Collomia* (Glue Plant)

1a—Lvs oblong, margins lobed. *C. heterophylla.*
1b—Lvs linear, and margins entire. See 2.

2a—Fls salmon-yellow. *C. grandiflora.*
2b—Fls pink or white. *C. linearis.*

The surface of *Collomia* seeds becomes thick and mucilaginous
when wet. Seeds of most species in California germinate with the
first fall rains and flower the following spring. It is thought that
the mucilaginous surface is a mechanism which helps store water
between the first fall rains that often come several weeks apart.
Once a seed starts to germinate it will perish if it dries out.
Many other plants use the same protective mechanism.

Collomia heterophylla—Variable-leaved Collomia. Plant much-branched, 5–20 cm tall; lvs toothed; fls bunched on branch tips, rose to white. W. slope below 4000. FW, MCF. April–June.

C. grandiflora—Grand-flowered Collomia. Fig. 83. Stem usually single, 1–10 dm tall; lvs linear; fls salmon-yellow in a terminal head. Dry open places below 8000, common. FW, C, MCF. April–July.

C. linearis—Narrow-leaved Collomia. Stem single, 1–6 dm tall; lvs linear; fls pink to white in terminal head. Dry places below 11000. MCF. May–Aug.

Key to the Genus *Phlox*

1a—Fls long tubular, 1–3 cm. *P. stansburyi.*
1b—Fls shorter, less than 1 cm long. See 2.

2a—Fls showy, perennial cushion plants. See 3.
2b—Fls tiny, annual plants. *Phlox gracilis.*

3a—Plant in a loose clump, low elevations. *P. speciosa.*
3b—Plants in dense low clumps, higher elevations. See 4.

4a—Hairs on plant not sticky. *P. diffusa.*
4b—Hairs on plant sticky, very low flat plants. (1–2 cm thick).
    P. covillei.

Phlox stansburyi—Stansbury's Phlox. Plant small, almost shrubby, in loose clumps; fls rose to whitish; corolla, long tubular, 2–3 cm long. Dry slopes amongst sage-brush on e. slope. PJ. April–June.

P. gracilis—Slender Phlox. Fig. 84. Annual. Plant small; stem slender, 1–2 dm tall; fls rose-purple, corolla with a yellowish tube, 8–12 mm long. Common in open grassy places below 10000. FW, C, MCF. March–Aug.

P. speciosa subsp. *occidentalis*—Western Showy Phlox. Pl. 7a. Plant semi-shrub, 2–4 dm tall; fls bright pink. Open hillsides below 7000 on w. slope. FW, PJ. April–June.

[92]

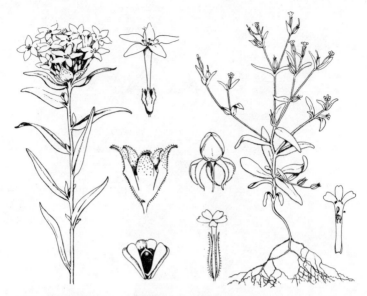

Fig. 83 *Collomia grandiflora*   Fig. 84 *Phlox gracilis*

P. diffusa—Spreading Phlox. Plant low, loosely branched, semi-shrub; fls lilac to pink. Frequent in open rocky places 3000 to Sierra crest. MCF, S, A. May–Aug.

Most common phlox in Sierra. Flowers soon after snow melts.

P. covillei—Coville's Phlox. Plant grows in flat carpets; lvs with sticky glandular hairs; fls pink, scattered about the carpet. Sierra crest and e. slope. A. May–July.

Named for Frederick Coville, who worked for the Smithsonian Institution and explored the West for plants. He headed the Death Valley Expedition in 1891.

Key to the Genus *Linanthus*

1a—Semi-shrubby plants. *L. nuttallii.*
1b—Low plants without woody base. See 2.

2a—Fls pure white, opening in evening. *L. dichotomus.*
2b—Fls mostly reddish, open all day. See 3.

3a—Lvs with a few short hairs. *L. bicolor.*
3b—Lvs with conspicuous hairs on margins. See 4.

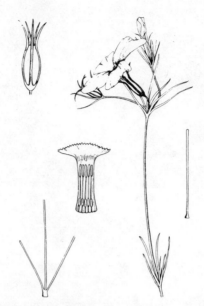

Fig. 85 *Linanthus dichotomus*

4a—Fls 12–25 mm long. *L. ciliatus*.
4b—Fls 25–30 mm long. *L. montanus*.

Linanthus nuttallii—Nuttall's Linanthus. Plant low, bushy; fls many, creamy white, corolla with yellow throat. Dry rocky slopes along e. slope. MCF, PJ. May–Aug.

L. dichotomus —Evening Snow. Fig. 85. Stem 1–2 dm tall; fls large, white, which open in early evening and close in morning. Grassy places at low elevations on w. slope. FW. April–June.

The white flower color and nectar attract night-flying moths, which pollinate this plant.

L. bicolor—Bicolored Linanthus. Pl. 6c. Stem 0.5–3 dm tall; 5–9 parted; fls in dense heads, corolla rose, white or yellowish with a yellow tube. Open places below 4000 on w. slope. FW, C. April–July.

L. ciliatus—Whisker Brush or Bristly-leaved Linanthus. Pl. 6g. Stem 1–3 dm tall; lvs 5–11 cleft with hairy

Fig. 86 *Navarretia viscidula*   Fig. 87 *Navarretia intertexta*

margins; fls rose to white, red dots on petals, yellow corolla throat. Dry open places below 8000 on both slopes of Sierra. FW, MCF. April–July.

L. montanus—Mustang Clover. Pl. 6e. Plant tall, 1–6 dm; lvs below fls with hairy margins; fls in terminal cluster, corolla pink or white with purple spot on each petal lobe, yellow throat. Dry slopes below 5000 on w. slope. FW. May–Aug.

Key to the Genus *Navarretia*

1a—Fls yellow. *N. breweri.*
1b—Fls blue to purple. See 2.

2a—Stem sticky. *N. viscidula.*
2b—Stem not sticky. See 3.

3a—Lvs divided into 3 narrow pinnate lobes, the central one 3–4
     times longer. *N. divaricata.*
3b—Lvs divided into many pinnatified lobes. *N. intertexta.*

Navarretia breweri—Brewer's Navarretia. (See p. 58).
Stem 2–12 cm tall, hairy, brown, slightly sticky; lvs pin-

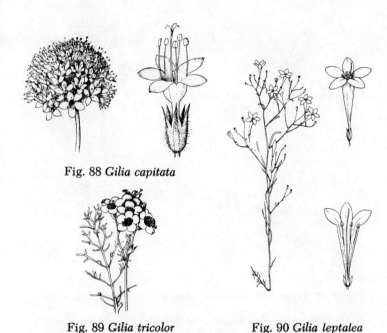

Fig. 88 *Gilia capitata*

Fig. 89 *Gilia tricolor*   Fig. 90 *Gilia leptalea*

natified, spiny; fls yellow. Semi-dry flats, 4000–11000 on e. slope. PJ, MCF. June–Aug.

N. viscidula subsp. *purpurea*—Sticky Navarretia. Fig. 86. Stem 3–15 cm tall, white or purplish, very sticky; lvs pinnatified, spiny; fls blue to purple. Dry open places below 4000 on w. slope. FW, C, YPF. June–July.

N. divaricata—Mountain Navarretia. Stem 3–15 cm tall, simple or divaricately branched; lf divided into 3 narrow lobes with the central one 3–4 times longer than the 2 side ones; fls pink to purple or white. Dry open areas, 3000–8500 on w. slope. YPF, MCF. June–Aug.

N. intertexta—Needle-leaved Navarretia. Fig. 87. Stems brown, hairy, 5–20 cm tall; fls pale blue to white. Moist hollows which dry out below 6000 on w. slope. FW, C. May–July.

Key to the Genus *Gilia*

1a—Lf pinnately dissected. See **2**.
1b—Lf linear. See 3.

2a—Fls in small round heads, violet to light blue. *G. capitata*.
2b—Fls in loose cyme, 3 colored. *G. tricolor*.

3a—Fls 8–18 mm long. *G. leptalea*.
3b—Fls 3–6 mm long. *G. capillaris*.

Gilia capitata—Blue Field Gilia Fig. 88. Stem 2–8 dm tall; lvs pinnate; fls 50–100, tiny, in round balls, light blue to violet. Very common in open areas below 7000 on w. slope. FW, C, MCF. April–July.

G. tricolor—Tricolor Gilia. Fig. 89. Stem much branched, 1–4 dm tall; fls 1–5 per branchlet, blue-violet, corolla tube yellow with 5 pairs of purple spots. Open grassy places below 4000 on w. slope. FW, C. March–April.

G. leptalea—Bridge's Gilia. Fig. 90. Stem 0.5–3.5 dm tall, more or less glandular throughout; lvs linear; fls pink to violet, 8–18 mm long. Openings in woods, 4500–10000, widespread especially on e. slope. MCF, PJ. June–Aug.

G. capillaris—Smooth-leaved Gilia. Stem 0.2–3 dm, branched; lvs linear throughout; fls pale violet to pink to white. Open sandy flats, 2500–7500, widespread. FW, C, MCF. June–Aug.

Genus *Ipomopsis*

Ipomopsis aggregata—Scarlet Trumpet Flower or Sky Trumpet. Fig. 91. Stems single, 3–8 dm tall; lvs pinnately dissected; fls long trumpetlike, bright pink to yellowish, color highly variable. Open areas from Sierra crest and along e. slope. MCF, S, A. June–Sept.

Indians valued this plant because they used it to make a tea to treat children's colds, to make glue, to treat blood troubles, to treat gonorrhea in a 5-day hot sweat process, and they extracted a blue dye from the roots.

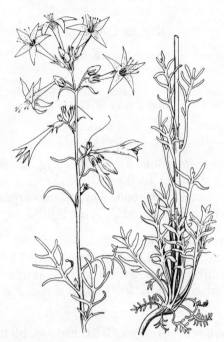

Fig. 91 *Ipomopsis aggregata*

Allophyllum violaceum—Violet Allophyllum. Stem 0.7–4 dm tall, glandular hairy; fls dark blue-violet, 2–3 fls per branchlet. Sandy places, 4000–8000, common. MCF. May–July.

KEY TO THE FAMILY HYDROPHYLLACEAE (WATERLEAF)

1a—All lvs entire, no toothing of any kind. See 2.
1b—Lvs pinnately divided or if entire, toothed. See 3.

2a—Cluster of lvs without stem. *Hesperochiron.*
2b—Stem obviously leafy. *Draperia.*

3a—Basal lvs alternate, stamens longer than petals. See 4.
3b—Basal lvs opposite, stamens same length as petals or shorter. See 5.

[98]

Fig. 92 *Draperia systyla*   Fig. 93 *Phacelia hydrophylloides*

4a—Lvs distributed along stem. *Phacelia.*
4b—Lvs mostly basal. *Hydrophyllum.*

5a—Stems rarely with thorny prickles. *Nemophila.*
5b—Stems with horny prickles. *Pholistoma.*

Key to the Genus *Hesperochiron*

1a—Fls flat to shallowly bowl-shaped. *H. pumilus.*
1b—Fls funnel-shaped. *H. californicus.*

The genus name is derived from two Greek words, *hesperus* =
western and *Chiron* = a centaur by that name.

Hesperochiron pumilus—Dwarf Hesperochiron. Plant
low to ground; lvs 2.5–5 cm long; fls white-bluish tint,
flat, 1–3 cm broad. Moist flats below 9000, common.
MCF. April–July.

H. californicus—California Hesperochiron. Plant low
to ground; lvs 1–5 cm long; fls funnel-like, white with
bluish tint. Moist places, 4000–9000, widespread. MCF.
May–July.

[99]

Genus *Draperia*

Draperia systyla—Draperia. Fig. 92. Stems few, 1–4 dm long; lvs ovate, 2.5–5 cm long, soft-hairy; fls with compact cymes, pale violet, tubular 10–14 mm long. Dry sandy places below 8000 on w. slope. MCF. April–June.

Named for J. W. Draper, an American historian.

Key to the Genus *Phacelia*

1a—Most of lvs entire. See 2.
1b—Lvs pinnatified. See 6.

2a—Petal edges rolled under. *P. hydrophylloides.*
2b—Petal edges flat. See 3.

3a—Fl stem usually more than 3 dm tall. *P. mutabilis.*
3b—Fl stem less than 2 dm tall. See 4.

4a—Lvs oval, skunklike odor. *P. quickii.*
4b—Lvs linear-oblong. See 5.

5a—Lvs hairy. *P. racemosa.*
5b—Lvs mostly hairless. *P. eisenii.*

6a—Fls dirty white. See 7.
6b—Fls blue-purple. See 8.

7a—Base of plant not woody. *P. cicutaria.*
7b—Base of plant woody. *P. ramosissima.*

8a—Fls blue. *P. distans.*
8b—Fls purplish with yellow corolla tube. *P. bicolor.*

Phacelia hydrophylloides—Waterleaf Phacelia. Fig. 93. Stems sprawling, 1–3 dm long; lvs oblong-ovate and coarsely toothed; fls violet-blue to whitish, margins of petal lobes rolled under. Dry open woods, 5000–10000 on w. slope. MCF. June–Aug.

P. mutabilis—Changeable Phacelia. Lvs in basal cluster, grayish-green, lanceolate-ovate, 2–8 cm long, changeable, some with 1–2 pairs of leaflets; fls lavender to whitish on leafless stem. Many places, 4000–10000. MCF. June–Aug.

The many variable leaf shapes have caused much confusion and the naming of many questionable species.

[100]

P. quickii—Quick's Phacelia. Stem simple or branched, 5–20 cm tall, skunklike odor; lvs oval; fls lavender-blue. Open sandy places, 4000–7200 on w. slope. MCF. May–June.

P. racemosa—Racemose Phacelia. Stem simple, slender, 5–20 cm tall; lower lvs opposite, lance-oblong; fls bluish, in loose racemose cymes. Dry places, 5000–9000, on w. slope north of Fresno Co. MCF. June–Aug.

P. eisenii—Eisen's Phacelia. Stems branched, slender, 3–15 cm tall; lower lvs opposite, linear; fls pale lavender, in short loosely arranged cymes. Rocky places, 4000–11000. MCF. June–Aug.

P. cicutaria—Caterpillar Phacelia. Stems 2–6 dm, erect or weak; lvs pinnate into sharply oblong divisions; fls dirty yellowish-white. Dry open slopes below 4000 on w. slope. FW, C. March–June.

P. ramosissima—Branching Phacelia. Stems coarse, 5–10 dm long, glandular-hairy; lvs pinnately lobed 4–10 cm long; fls dirty white to bluish. Rocky places below 9000, widespread. MCF. May–July.

P. distans—Common Phacelia or Wild Heliotrope. Stem 2–8 dm tall, branched to sprawling; lvs pinnate into oblong divisions; fls blue. Many places below 7000. FW, C, MCF. March–June.

P. bicolor—Two-colored Phacelia. Stems 0.5–4 dm tall, branched from a common base; lvs pinnatified into linear divisions; fls purplish with yellow corolla tube, 9–16 mm long. Sandy places below 10000 on e. slope. MCF, SS. May–Aug.

Genus *Hydrophyllum*

Hydrophyllum occidentale—California Waterleaf. Fig. 94. Stem somewhat sprawling, 1–6 dm long; lvs pinnate; fls whitish to violet in cymose clusters, 7–10 mm long. Dry shaded woods below 9000. MCF. May–July.

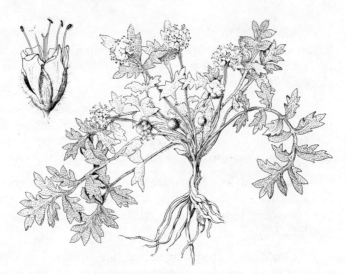

Fig. 94 *Hydrophyllum occidentale*

Key to the Genus *Nemophila*

1a—Fls 1–4 cm broad. See 2.
1b—Fls less than 1 cm broad. See 3.

2a—Fls light blue. *N. menziesii.*
2b—Fls white with large purple spots. *N. maculata.*

3a—Fls light blue. *N. pulchella.*
3b—Fls white. See 4.

4a—Lvs pinnately divided. *N. heterophylla.*
4b—Lvs spatulalike. *N. spatulata.*

The genus name is derived from the two Greek words, *nemo* = grove and *phila* = to love.

Nemophila menziesii—Baby Blue Eyes. Stem sprawling, 1–3 dm long; fls light blue. Usually in large masses in moist open meadows below 5000 on w. slope during spring. FW, C, MM. Feb–June.

N. maculata—Fivespot. Pl. 7*h.* Stems sprawling, 1–3 dm long; fls with each petal white with a large purple spot at the base. Moist flats below 7500 on w. slope, common. FW, C, YPF. April–July.

[102]

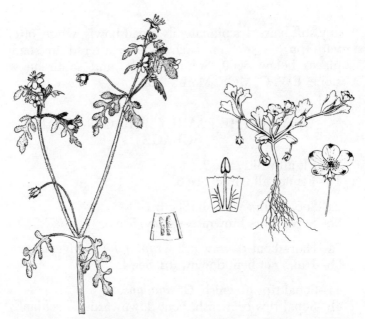

Fig. 95 *Nemophila pulchella*   Fig. 96 *Nemophila spatulata*

N. pulchella—Pretty Nemophila. Fig. 95. Stems weak, 1–4 dm long; lvs pinnately divided; fls small, light blue, 5–10 mm wide. Frequent on semishaded slopes below 6000 on w. slope. FW, C, MCF. April–June.

N. heterophylla—Variable-leaved Nemophila. Stem 1–3 dm tall; lvs usually pinnately divided or entire on same plant; fls white or bluish, 5–10 mm wide. Semishade below 5000 on w. slope. FW, C, MCF. March–July.

N. spatulata—Sierra Nemophila. Fig. 96. Stems weak, 1–2 dm long; lvs spoon-shaped with 3 toothed edges; fls white or bluish. Damp shade, 4000–10500, mostly on w. slope. MCF. May–July.

Genus *Pholistoma*

Pholistoma membranaceum—White Fiesta Flower. Stems weak, 2–5 dm long, waxy surface and occasionally stiff hairs; lvs pinnate; fls broad bowls, white, often with purple spot on each lobe. Scattered in shady places below 5000, Stanislaus Co. and south on w. slope. FW, C, MCF. March–May.

KEY TO THE FAMILY BORAGINACEAE
(BORAGE)

1a—Fls all white. See 2.
1b—Fls not all white. See 6.

2a—Sepal hairs whitish. See 3.
2b—Sepal hairs brownish-yellow. See 5.

3a—Hairs bent downward. *Cryptantha nubigena.*
3b—Hairs not bent downward. See 4.

4a—Sepal tips greenish. *C. simulans.*
4b—Sepal tips brownish, bent downward. *C. echinella.*

5a—Lower lvs opposite. *Plagiobothrys hispidulus.*
5b—Lower lvs alternate. *P. nothofulvus.*

6a—Fls with some blue. See 7.
6b—Fls yellow-orange. *Amsinckia intermedia.*

7a—Petal tips parallel to fl tube. *Mertensia.*
7b—Petal tips at right angles to fl tube. See 8.

8a—Fls dark blue. *Cynoglossum grande.*
8b—Fls pale blue or whitish-yellow throat. See 9.

9a—Lvs long, linear. *Hackelia jessicae.*
9b—Lvs ovate, high alpine. *H. sharsmithii.*

Genus *Cryptantha*

The genus name is from two Greek words, *cryptos* = hidden and *anthos* = flower. The lilac-colored (with yellow, black and white lines) caterpillars of the Painted Lady Butterfly use members of the *Cryptantha* genus as a food plant.

Cryptantha nubigena–Sierra Cryptantha. Pl. 7c. Plant

with dense leafy base, 0.5–1.5 dm tall, hairs bent downward, these mixed with large bristles; sepals long and slender; fls in dense spikelike heads. Open places 8000–125000, frequent. S, A. July–Aug.

C. simulans—Pine Cryptantha. Stems with a few ascending branches, 1–4 dm tall, covered with dense whitish hairs, stiff and sharp; sepals lance-linear with spreading green tips, midrib with brownish bristles. Semi-open woods, 2500–7500, on w. slope. PP, MCF. May–July.

C. echinella—Prickly Cryptantha. Stem erect, sparsely branched, 0.5–3 dm, short-hirsute haired; sepals oblong-ovoid spreading with tips bent downward. Open places below 9000, common. FW, C, PP, MCF. June–Aug.

Genus *Plagiobothrys*

The Indians used the stem base and roots of some *Plagiobothrys* species to obtain a rouge.

Plagiobothrys hispidulus—Harsh Plagiobothrys. Stem grayish-green, 0.5–4 dm tall; lvs linear. 1–5 cm long; fls 2–3 mm long. Flats, 4000–11000. MM. June–Sept.

P. nothofulvus—Popcorn Flower. Stem 2–5 cm tall; lvs linear, mostly in a basal cluster; fls 6–8 mm long, white. Very common in open fields below 4000 on w. slope. FW, C, MM. March–June.

Genus *Amsinckia*

Amsinckia intermedia—Fiddleneck. Pl. 7*b*. Plant much branched, 2–8 dm tall; fls many, orange-yellow, 8–10 mm, in a distinctive curved cyme. Common, often in great masses in disturbed places below 5000. FW, C, MM. Feb–May.

A food plant for the Painted Lady Butterfly.

Fig. 97 *Mertensia ciliata*   Fig. 98 *Cynoglossum grande*

Genus *Mertensia*

Mertensia ciliata var. *stomatechoides*—Mountain Blue Bells or Lungwort. Fig. 97. Stems 5–15 dm tall, usually in clumps; fls many, blue-purple, 1–2 cm long, with petals parallel to fl tube. Dry open meadows, 5000–10500. MM. May–Aug.

Genus *Cynoglossum*

The generic name is derived from the Greek words *cyno* = dog and *glossum* = tongue. A good hunting dog is supposed to have a bluish tongue like the flowers of this genus.

Cynoglossum grande—Grand Hound's Tongue. Fig. 98. Stem 2–4 dm tall; lvs hairy, oblanceolate, 5–15 cm long; fls blue, tinged brown or pink, 0.5–1 cm long. Openings in woods below 7000 on w. slope. FW, C, MCF. May–July.

C. occidentale—Similar to *C. grande*, but with oblanceolate lvs.

Genus *Hackelia*

Hackelia jessicae—Jessica's Stickseed. Stem 3–6 dm tall;

[106]

Fig. 99 *Nicotiana attenuata*   Fig. 100 *Datura meteloides*

lvs linear, 7–15 cm long; fls pale blue, 4–6 mm wide. Common in moist places, 4500–11000. MM. July–Aug.

H. sharsmithii—Sharsmith's Stickseed. Stem 1–3 dm tall; lvs oval, 1.5–4 cm long; fls bluish to white with a yellow center. Found at the base of rocky ledges in southern Sierra, 10500–12000. A. July–Sept.

Named for Carl Sharsmith, who studied the alpine flora of the Sierra for many years.

KEY TO THE FAMILY SOLANACEAE (NIGHTSHADE)

1a—Slender tubed fls. *Nicotiana attenuata*.
1b—Wide tubed fls. *Datura meteloides*.

Genus *Nicotiana*

Nicotiana attenuata—Coyote Tobacco. Fig. 99. Stems slender, 2–19 dm tall; lvs lance-ovate, 5–15 cm long, significantly glandular; fls white, with long slender trumpetlike corolla tubes, 2.5–3 cm. Disturbed places and particularly common the year after a forest fire, below 10000. MCF, MM, C, PJ. May–Oct.

Indians smoked the leaves, but even after various treatments it is strong and harsh when compared to commercial tobacco, which is a different species.

Genus *Datura*

Datura meteloides—Jimson Weed. Fig. 100. Plants large, much-branched, 5–10 dm tall; lvs ovate, 4–12 cm long, covered with minute grayish hairs; fls large, white, trumpet-shaped, 15–18 cm long. Many scattered places, often along roads. FW, C, MCF, SS. June–Oct.

Indians made a solution from the leaves to wash a horse that "wants to stray"; supposedly the horse will not stray after treatment. Poisonous to man.

KEY TO THE FAMILY SCROPHULARIACEAE (FIGWORT)

1a—Fls nearly regular, 5 pollen producing stamens. *Verbascum.*

1b—Fls long tubed and 2–lipped, 2 or 4 pollen producing stamens. See 2.

2a—Stigma flattened into 2 lips. *Mimulus.*
2b—Stigma enlarged or flattened but not 2–lipped. See 3.

3a—Lvs undivided, top tip of fl corolla tube not enlarged. See 4.
3b—Some of lvs 1–5-parted, fl corolla tube narrow with upper tip enlarged as a bulge or hook. See 7.

---

1 millimeter
10 millimeters = 1 centimeter = 13/32 inch
10 centimeters = 1 decimeter = ca. 4 inches
10 decimeters = 1 meter = 3.3 feet

Fig. 101 Metric scale 1:1

4a—Fl corolla tube base swollen on upper side. *Collinsia*.

4b—Base of fl corolla tube not swollen. See 5.

5a—Upper lip of fl appearing as 1 lobe. *Veronica*.

5b—Upper lip of fl 2-lobed. See 6.

6a—Lvs triangular, with edges regularly saw-toothed. *Scrophularia*.

6b—Lvs and fls not as above. *Penstemon*.

7a—Lvs pinnate. *Pedicularis*.

7b—Lvs 1–5-parted. See 8.

8a—Lower lip of fl enlarged into 3 sacs. *Orthocarpus*.

8b—Lower lip of fl not enlarged. *Castilleja*.

Key to the Genus *Verbascum*
(Mullein)

1a—Entire plant white-wooly. *V. thapsus*.

1b—Entire plant green. *V. blattaria*.

Verbascum thapsus—Common Mullein. Pl. 7*e*. Stem stout, unbranched, 5–18 dm tall; most lvs basal; entire plant white-wooly; fls many, small, yellow, in terminal spike. Frequent along roads and abandoned fields. FW, C, MCF, MM, SS. June–Sept.

Introduced from Eurasia.

V. blattaria—Moth Mullein. Stem slender, unbranched, 4–12 dm tall; lvs green; fls all yellow or white. Frequent weed in dry open places below 4000. FW, C, MCF. June–Aug.

Introduced from Eurasia.

Key to the Genus *Mimulus* (Monkey Flower)

1a—Plants with a strong odor. See 2.

1b—Plants without a strong odor. See 3.

2a—Strong tobaccolike odor. *M. bolanderi*.

2b—Strong skunklike odor. *M. mephiticus*.

3a—Plants sprawling in wet places, rooting along stem. See 4.
3b—Plant erect, moist to dry places. See 8.

4a—Fls yellow. See 5.
4b—Fls red to pink. See 7.

5a—Fls all yellow, stem slimy. *M. moschatus.*
5b—Fls with colored spots. See 6.

6a—Fl pedicel short and thick. *M. guttatus.*
6b—Fl pedicel long threadlike. *M. primuloides.*

7a—Fls scarlet. *M. cardinalis.*
7b—Fls rose to pink. *M. lewisii.*

8a—Fls mostly yellow. *M. suksdorfii.*
8b—Fls purple to pink or white. See 9.

9a—Plant erect, 0.5–4 dm tall. See 10.
9b—Plant tufted, less than 0.3 dm tall. See 12.

10a—Fls white, lower lip yellow and red dotted. *M. bicolor.*
10b—Fls pink to purple. See 11.

11a—Fls purple to wine red, dry places. *M. torreyi.*
11b—Fls pale pink to purple, moist places. *M. breweri.*

12a—Fls long tubular, yellow within. *M. angustatus.*
12b—Fls long tubular, rose purple within. *M. kelloggii.*

The genus name is from the Latin word *minus* = comic actor, because the flowers have grinning "faces" like an early-day comic actor. In some species the two-lipped stigma closes immediately when touched lightly. This is believed to be a mechanism to prevent self-pollination; when a bee enters a flower for nectar the pollen of that particular flower cannot pollinate itself as the bee brushes by the closed stigma as it exits. Cross-pollination is thus ensured.

Mimulus bolanderi—Bolander's Monkey Flower. Fig. 102. Stem 2–6 dm tall, strong tobaccolike odor; fls pink to red-purple. Disturbed dry open places on w. slope below 6500. FW, C, MCF, MM. May–July.

Named for Henry Bolander, who made extensive botanical collections from 1863–1875 while working on the California State Geological Survey with William Brewer.

M. mephiticus—Skunky Monkey Flower. Stem 0.2–

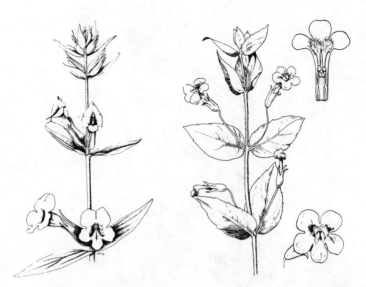

Fig. 102 *Mimulus bolanderi*   Fig. 103 *Mimulus moschatus*

1.2 dm tall, strong skunklike odor; fls yellow streaked with red. Common in sandy places, 5000–9000. MCF, MM. June–Aug.

M. moschatus–Musk Monkey Flower. Fig. 103. Stem 0.5–3 dm tall, creeping, has slimy feeling; fls yellow, 18–26 mm long. Wet places below 7500 on w. slope. FW, C, MCF, MM. June–Aug.

M. guttatus–Common Monkey Flower. Fig. 104. Stems quite variable from very short to 10 dm tall, creeping and rooting along stem; fls yellow, spotted red. The most common mimulus in wet places below 10000. FW, C, MCF, MM. March–Aug.

Indians ate the slightly bitter leaves and stems as greens. They also crushed the leaves and used them as a poultice for rope burns. The caterpillars of both the Sierra Checker Spot and Buckeye butterflies feed on *M. guttatus*.

M. primuloides–Primrose Monkey Flower. Fig. 105. Lvs in small, low cluster with very long threadlike pedicels; fls yellow, spotted with red-brown. Often in

[111]

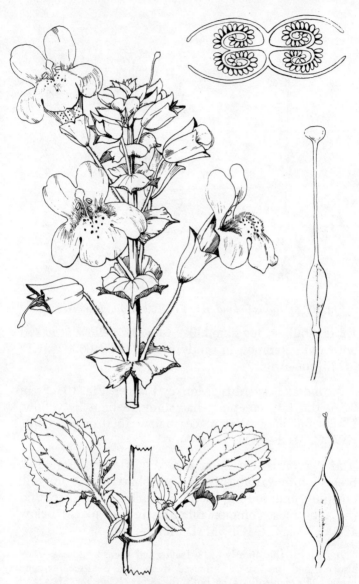

Fig. 104 *Mimulus guttatus*

masses on wet banks 4000–8000. MCF, MM. June–Aug.

M. cardinalis–Scarlet Monkey Flower. Stem 2.5–8 dm tall; fls scarlet. Wet stream banks and springy

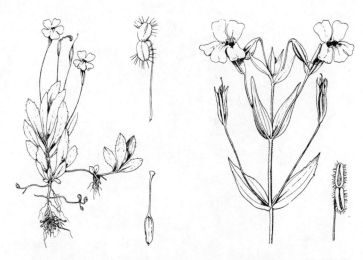

Fig. 105 *Mimulus primuloides*   Fig. 106 *Mimulus lewisii*

places below 8000, mostly on w. slope. FW, C, MCF.
April–Oct.

M. lewisii—Lewis's or Great Purple Monkey Flower.
Fig. 106. (See p. 68.) Stem 3–8 dm tall; fls rose to pink.
Wet stream banks, 4000–10000. MCF. June–Aug.

M. suksdorfii—Sukdorf's Monkey Flower. Stems compact, bushy, 0.1–0.6 dm tall; fls yellow, faintly brown
spotted, 5–6 mm long. Moist sandy places 5000–13000
along Sierra crest and e. slope. PJ, MCF, S, A. May–
Aug.

Named for Wilhelm Suksdorf, an amateur botanist of the
Pacific Northwest, who knew the plants as well as professional
botanists.

M. bicolor—Yellow and White Monkey Flower. Stem
1–3 dm tall; fls 1–6, upper petals white, lower yellow
with red dots. Moist meadows below 6000 on w. slope.
FW, C, MCF. April–June.

M. torreyi—Torrey's Monkey Flower. Pl. 7g. Fig. 107.
Stems 0.5–3.5 dm tall; fls wine-red, 1.5–2.2 cm long,
yellow ridges within fl tube. Frequent in dry undis-

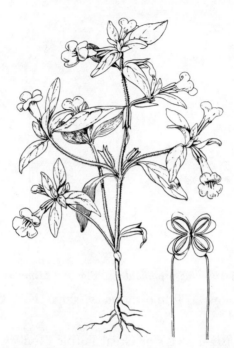

Fig. 107 *Mimulus torreyi*

turbed places below 8000. FW, C, MCF, MM. May–Aug.

Named for John Torrey a professor at Columbia College, New York, who studied many of the collections sent east by the explorers of the early and mid-1800s.

M. breweri–Brewer's Monkey Flower. (See p. 58.) Stems 0.5–1.8 dm tall; fls pale pink to purplish with yellow ridges within. Widespread in damp sandy places 4000–11000. MCF, MM, S. June–Aug.

M. angustatus–Pansy Monkey Flower. Pl. 7f. Plant small, tufted, 0.1–0.3 dm tall; each fl a long yellowish trumpetlike corolla tube, 2–5 cm long, throat and lips a light purple with maroon dots. In moist, recently dried depressions in open areas below 5000 on w. slope. MM. May–July.

M. kelloggii–Kellogg's Monkey Flower. (See p. 76.)

[114]

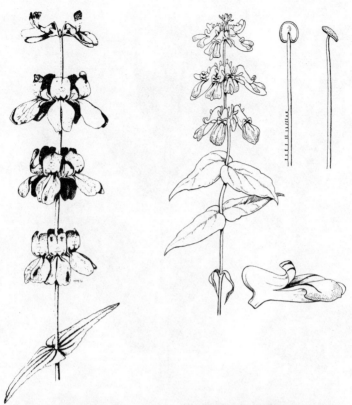

Fig. 108 *Collinsia heterophylla*   Fig. 109 *Collinsia tinctoria*

Plant small, tufted like *M. pulchellus,* but fl long rose-purple trumpetlike corolla tube, lips purple and yellow with red dots. In recently dried depressions below 4000 on w. slope. MM. March–June.

Key to the Genus *Collinsia*

1a—Fls white and deep violet. *C. heterophylla.*
1b—Fls with some yellow. See 2.

2a—Stems short 0.5–1.5 dm tall. *C. torreyi.*
2b—Stems taller, 2–6 dm tall. *C. tinctoria.*

The genus is named for Zaccheus Collins, a botanist of early America.

Fig. 110 *Veronica americana*

Collinsia heterophylla—Chinese Houses. Pl. 7*d*. Fig. 108. Stems 2–5 dm tall; fls tubular, 1.5–2 cm long, with upper lip white to lilac and lower lip violet, arranged in dense whorls. Common in shaded woods below 4000 on w. slope. FW, C. March–June.

C. torreyi — Torrey's Collinsia. (See p. 114.) Stem small, highly branched, 0.5–2 im tall; fl with upper lip of pale white with yellow base and purple dots, lower lip deep blue. Widespread in moist sandy flats below 10000. FW, C, MCF, MM. May–Aug.

C. tinctoria—Tincture Plant. Fig. 109. Stems branched, 2–6 dm tall, usually many plants in a mass

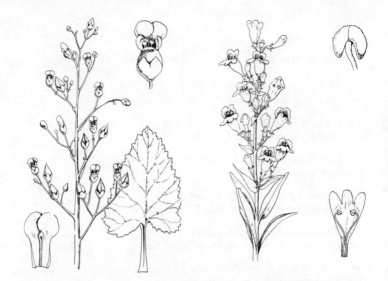

Fig. 111 *Scrophularia californica*   Fig. 112 *Penstemon laetus*

giving the field a light yellow color from the fls; corolla tube purple dotted. Open places below 6000 on w. slope. FW, C, MCF. May–Aug.

The crushed leaves or stems will stain one's hands a yellowish brown.

Genus *Veronica*

Veronica americana—Speedwell. Fig. 110. Stems 1–3 dm tall; lvs oblong-oval, 5–15 mm; fls white to light blue, 6–7 mm wide, upper 2 petal lobes fused into 1, giving a 4-lobed appearance. Wet springy places below 12000. FW, MCF, S, A. June–Aug.

The leaves and stems used to be eaten in salads. They are a source of vitamin C, which prevents scurvy.

Genus *Scrophularia*

Scrophularia californica—Bee Plant. Fig. 111. Stems coarse, 1–2 m tall; lvs triangular, 3–10 cm long, edges saw-toothed; fl a short gaping corolla tube of red-brown to maroon. Common in damp brushy thickets below 5000. FW, C, MCF. Feb–Aug.

Indians obtained a black dye from this species. The Sierra Checker Spot Butterfly caterpillar feeds on Bee Plants.

[117]

Key to the Genus *Penstemon* (Bearded Tongue)

1a—Fls blue-purple. See 2.
1b—Fls red to white. See 9.

2a—Anthers hairless or nearly so. See 3.
2b—Anthers densely white-wooly. *P. davidsonii*.

3a—Lvs oblanceolate to ovate. See 4.
3b—Lvs linear. See 5.

4a—Flowering stem sticky. *P. laetus*.
4b—Flowering stem not sticky. *P. azureus*.

5a—Flowering stem sticky and hairy. See 6.
5b—Flowering stem not sticky or hairy. See 7.

6a—Lvs hairless. *P. heterodoxus*.
6b—Lvs minutely hairy. *P. humilis*.

7a—Fl corolla 18–35 mm long. *P. speciosus*.
7b—Fl corolla tube shorter, 7–18 mm long. See 8.

8a—Fl corolla tube 7–10 mm long, bent downward. *P. procerus*.
8b—Fl corolla tube 10–15 mm, horizontal. *P. rydbergii*.

9a—Fls bright red, somewhat shrubby. *P. bridgesii*.
9b—Fls rose to deep pink. *P. newberryi*.

There are about 230 species in the *Penstemon* genus, and most are strikingly beautiful. Indians had many uses for them: eyewash from a solution of soaked leaves, tea as a laxative, powdered leaves and roots for sores, and raw leaf-juice to wash venereal disease sores. Even casual observation of the different bees and hummingbirds that visit flowers of this genus will show that each species of *Penstemon* has a specific pollinator. This is one of nature's ways of preventing hybridization between species. Caterpillars of the Sierra Checkerspot Butterfly use this genus as food plants.

Penstemon davidsonii—Davidson's Penstemon. Pl. 8a. Plants woody branched mats; lvs elliptic to roundish; fl stem 1 dm tall; fls purple-violet, 18–35 mm long, anthers white wooly. Common in dry rocky places along ridge crests, 9000–12000. S, A. July–Aug.

P. laetus—Gay Penstemon. Fig. 112. Plant woody at base, 2–8 dm tall; lvs oblanceolate and gray or yellow-green; fl stem sticky; fl corolla tube 20–30 mm long, blue-lavender with a gaping (wide) corolla tube opening. Dry rocky places below 8500 on w. slope. FW, C, MCF. May–July.

P. azureus—Azure Penstemon. Plant with woody base; stems 2–5 dm tall; lvs oblanceolate to ovate, bluish waxy surface; fl stem not sticky; fl corolla tube 20–30 mm long, blue violet. Dry rocky slopes below 7500. FW, C, MCF. May–Aug.

P. heterodoxus—Sierra Penstemon. Stems slender, 1–2 dm tall; lvs linear in basal cluster, deep green, hairless; fls in dense sticky clusters, blue-purple, 10–16 mm long. Common in open places, 8000–12000. MCF, MM, S, A. July–Aug.

P. humilus—Lowly Penstemon. Stems in tufted cushion, 1–3 dm tall; lvs linear with minute grayish hairs; fl stem sticky; fls azure-blue, 12–16 mm long. Lower dry slopes on e. slope. PJ. May–July.

P. speciosus—Showy Penstemon. Pl. 8g. Stems clumped 2–8 dm tall; lvs linear sometimes with waxy blue surface; fls 25–35 mm long, bright blue-purple. Dry loose soils, 3500–8000. MCF, S. June–Aug.

P. procerus subsp. *formosus*—Small-flowered Penstemon. Stems densely tufted, 0.4–1.5 dm long; lvs deep green in a basal cluster, hairless; fls deep blue-purple, 7.5–11 mm long, in tight clusters. Rocky meadows 6500–11000. MM. July–Aug.

P. rydbergii—Rydberg's Meadow Penstemon. Pl. 8b. Stems slender, 2–7 dm tall; lvs bright green in basal cluster, linear; fls 1–6 in distinct clusters, blue-purple, 1–14 mm long. Meadows, 4600–8100. MM. May–Aug.

Named for Per Axel Rydberg, an engineer who collected bo-

Fig. 113 *Penstemon newberryi*   Fig. 114 *Pedicularis semi-barbata*

tanical specimens as a special interest. Eventually he devoted full time to botany and in 1922 wrote the first flora of the Rocky Mountains, based on his extensive exploring and collecting.

P. bridgesii—Bridges Penstemon. Plant with woody base; stems 3–10 dm tall; fls bright red. Common on e. slope and less so on w. slope, 5000–11000. PJ, MCF, MM. June–Aug.

P. newberryi—Mountain Pride or Newberry's Penstemon. Fig. 113. (See p. 86.) Plant is low woody mat over boulders; fls rose to deep pink. MCF, S. 5000–11000.

Flowers soon after the snow melts.

Key to the Genus *Pedicularis* (Lousewort)

1a—Fls deep purple-red. *P. densiflora.*
1b—Fls pink or yellowish. See 2.

2a—Fls yellowish. *P. semibarbata.*
2b—Fls pink. See 3.

3a—Fl stem with many long wooly hairs. *P. attolens.*
3b—Fl stem hairless. *P. groenlandica.*

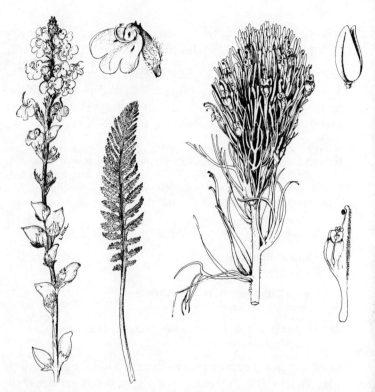

Fig. 115 *Pedicularis attolens*   Fig. 116 *Orthocarpus purpur-rascens*

Pedicularis densiflora—Indian Warrior. Fig. 114. Plant is usually a cluster of stems 1–5 dm tall; lvs pinnate, mostly basal; fls purple-red, many on each stem. Semi-shaded woods along w. slope below 4000. FW, C, PP. March–April.

P. semibarbata—Pine Woods Lousewort. Plant is low cluster of pinnate lvs to 1 dm tall; fls yellowish, parrot-beaked, with purplish tips. Common in dry shaded woods, 4000–11000. MCF. May–June.

P. attollens—Little Elephant's Head. Fig. 115. Stem 1.5–4 dm tall; lvs pinnate; fl stem with white-wooly hairs; fls pink with appearance of an elephant's head

[121]

with a short snout (3–6 mm long stigma). Common in moist meadows, 5000–12000. MM, S, A. June–Sept.

P. groenlandica—Elephant's Head. Pl. 8*f*. Stems 3–6 dm tall, hairless; lvs pinnate; fls red-purple with a long elephant snout (6–12 mm stigma). Very wet meadows, 6000–12000. MM, S, A. June–Aug.

This species and *P. attolens* often grow near each other, although *P. groenlandica* appears to require a much wetter habitat. Both species are pollinated by the same bumblebee, but the two flower shapes are different enough so that pollen adheres to a different part of the bee's body and thus no hybrids can occur.

Key to the Genus *Orthocarpus* (Owl's Clover)

1a—Fls rose-purple. See 2.
1b—Fls yellow. See 3.

2a—Lower fl lip 3-saced. *O. purpurascens.*
2b—Lower fl lip 1-saced. *O. copelandii.*

3a—Fls bright yellow, lower surface hairy. *O. lacerus.*
3b—Fls pale yellow-white, hairless. *O. hispidus.*

Orthocarpus purpurascens—Purple Owl's Clover. Fig. 116. Bracts and fls mostly purple in dense spikes. Frequent on w. slope below 4000. FW, C, MCF, MM. March–May.

The great purple masses of wildflowers one sees in spring and early summer are this species.

O. copelandii—Copeland's Owl's Clover. Stems 1–3.5 dm, finely haired; lvs mostly entire; fls rose-purple with white lower lip. Mostly on e. slope. MM, MCF, June–July.

Named for Edwin Copeland, who was a research botanist at the University of California.

O. lacerus—Cut-leaved Owl's Clover. Fig. 117. Stems slender; fls bright yellow. Grassy places below 6000 on w. slope. FW, C, MCF, MM. May–July.

O. hispidus—Hairy Owl's Clover. Stems slender; fls

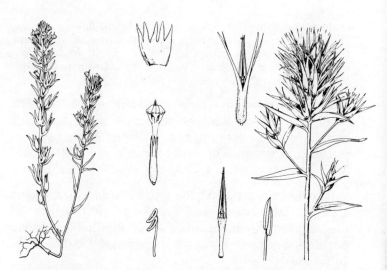

Fig. 117 *Orthocarpus lacerus*   Fig. 118 *Castilleja miniata*

pale yellow to white. Grassy meadows, 3000–7000 on w. slope. MM. May–Aug.

Key to the Genus *Castilleja* (Indian Paint Brush)

1a—Lower fl corolla lip ½ to as long as upper lip, often whitish. See 2.
1b—Lower fl corolla lip less than half as long as upper lip, usually greenish. See 3.

2a—Fl corolla 18–20 mm long. *C. lemmonii*.
2b—Fl corolla tube 13–16 mm long. *C. nana*.

3a—Lvs grayish to white wooly, hairs branched. *C. pruinosa*.
3b—Lvs green to grayish green, hairs not branched. See 4.

4a—Plants sticky-hairy below fls. See 5.
4b—Plants not as above. See 6.

5a—Stems more than 2 dm tall. *C. applegatei*.
5b—Stems less than 2 dm tall. *C. breweri*.

6a—Lower lvs not divided, 4–8 dm tall. *C. miniata*.
6b—Lower lvs with 1–2 pairs of lobes, 1–2 dm tall. *C. chromosa*.

Because Indian Paint Brush is often found growing among rocks, Indians called it "Snake's Friend." They thought that the

[123]

rattlesnake obtained its venom from the bright flowers. On the other hand, Indians also made a love potion from it! The Sierra Checkerspot Butterfly caterpillar feeds on Paint Brushes. *Castilleja* is the state flower of Wyoming. Hybrids often occur between species so that identification may be difficult.

Castilleja lemmonii—Lemmon's Paint Brush. Pl. 8*d*. Stem 1–2 dm tall; bracts and sepal tips purple; fl corolla tubes 18–20 mm long, hairy on back, margins purplish. Common in moist meadows, 7000–12000. MM. July–Aug.

C. nana—Dwarf or Alpine Paint Brush. Pl. 8*e*. Stems 1–2 dm tall; bracts and sepal tips dull yellow to purplish-red; fl corolla tubes 13–16 mm long, margins purplish. Frequent in alpine meadows, 8000–12000. A. July–Aug.

C. pruinosa—Gray Paint Brush. Stem 3–7 dm tall; stem and lvs grayish, hairs branched; bracts and sepals scarlet, tipped with yellow; fl corolla tube 25–30 mm long, yellowish with thin red margins. Dry rocky places below 8000 on w. slope. FW, C, MCF. April–Aug.

C. applegatei—Wavy-leaved Paint Brush. Stems 2–5 dm tall from woody base, sticky hairs; lvs wavy margined; bracts and sepals scarlet to yellowish; fl corolla tube 20–30 mm long with red margins. Frequent in dry places, 2000–11000. FW, C, MCF, S. May–Aug.

Named for Elmer Applegate, who is best known for his knowledge of the southern Oregon flora.

C. breweri — Brewer's Paint Brush. (See p. 58.) Stems 1–2 dm tall in clumps, sticky hairs; bracts and sepal tips a bright pinkish-red fl corolla tubes 16–22 mm long, top and bottoms greenish with red margins. Common in masses on meadows, 7000–11000. MM, S, A. June–Aug.

C. miniata—Great Red Paint Brush. Fig. 118. Stems few, 4–8 dm tall; bracts and sepal tips scarlet; fl corolla tube 25–35 mm long, reddish margins. Common along streams and wet places below 11000. MCF. May–Sept.

C. chromosa—Desert Paint Brush. Pl. 8c. Stems 1–4 dm tall from woody base; lower lvs with 1–2 pairs of lobes, hairs not branched; bracts and sepals a bright scarlet; fl corolla tubes 25–30 mm with wide reddish margins, lower tip dark green. Common at 2000–8000 on e. slope in sagebrush. PJ. April–Aug.

KEY TO THE FAMILY LABIATAE (MINT)

1a—Fls in dense terminal heads or spikes. See 2.
1b—Fls loosely arranged along fl stem. See 6.

2a—Fls white. *Marrubium vulgare.*
2b—Fls rose to purple. See 3.

3a—Fls in dense rounded head. *Monardella.*
3b—Fls in elongated head or spike. See 4.

4a—Fertile stamens, 2. *Salvia sonomensis.*
4b—Fertile stamens (pollen bearing), 4. See 5.

5a—Fls light rose. *Agastache urticifolia.*
5b—Fls bluish to purple. *Prunella vulgaris.*

6a—Lvs white-haired. See 7.
6b—Lvs nearly hairless, green. See 8.

7a—Fls blue. *Trichostemma oblongum.*
7b—Fls white to pinkish. *Stachys albens.*

8a—Fls blue. *Scutellaria tuberosa.*
8b—Fls white. *S. californica.*

Genus *Marrubium*

Marrubium vulgare—Horehound. Pl. 9a. Stems in clumps 2–6 dm tall; lvs and stem white-wooly; fls many whorls of small white fls in spikes. Common in disturbed places. FW, MCF. All year.

Fig. 119 *Agastache urticifolia*   Fig. 120 *Scutellaria tuberosa*

Introduced from Europe. Candy made from horehound is an old-fashioned treatment for sore throat.

Genus *Monardella*

Monardella odoratissima—Mountain Monardella or Coyote Mint. Plant much-branched, woody at base, 1.5–3.5 dm tall; lvs linear; fls pale purple in dense rounded heads, strong minty odor. In semi-shade below 11000. MCF. June–Aug.

Indians made a tea from the flowerheads which was used to help regulate the menstrual cycle of young women, as a treatment for colds, and as an appetizer drink.

Genus *Salvia*

Salvia sonomensis—Creeping Sage. Plant a creeping

mat of light gray-green lvs, easily recognized through-out year; fls blue-violet on leafless stems, 1–4 dm tall. Dry semi-shade of shrubs below 6500 on w. slope. FW, C. May–June.

Leaves have a strong odor if crushed.

Genus *Agastache*

Agastache urticifolia—Nettle-leaved Horse Mint. Fig. 119. Stems tall, 1–2 m; lvs ovate, 3.5–8 cm long; fls light rose in mass of brushlike spikes, 4 pollen-bearing sta-mens per fl. Moist to dry semi-open areas below 10000. MCF, S. June–Aug.

Plants have a strong unpleasant odor. The seeds can be made into a flour.

Genus *Prunella*

Prunella vulgaris—Selfheal. Stems a tufted mass, 1–5 dm tall; fls bluish to purple in dense spike with purplish tipped sepals. Semi-shaded woods below 5000 on w. slope. FW, C, MCF. May–Sept.

A delicious mintlike drink can be made by steeping fresh leaves in cold water.

Genus *Trichostemma*

Trichostemma oblongum—Mountain Blue Curls. Stem 1–4 dm tall, covered with soft white hairs; fls blue, 5–6 mm long. Dry edges of meadows below 10000 on w. slope. MM. June–Sept.

Indians mashed the plants for use as a fish stunner.

Genus *Stachys*

Stachys albens—White Hedge Nettle. Stem stout, 3–10 dm tall; lvs ovate, densely white-wooly; fls in loose spikes, white to pinkish, 6–8 mm long. Moist places be-low 8000 on both e. and w. slopes. FW, C, MCF. May–Oct.

Indians made a wash or poultice from soaked leaves to treat sores or wounds.

Genus *Scutellaria*

Scutellaria tuberosa—Blue Skullcap. Fig. 120. Roots tuberous; stem branched and sticky, 0.5–2 dm tall; lvs ovate 1–2 cm long; fls blue 15–20 mm long. Semi-shade along edge of woods below 5000 on w. slope. FW, C, MCF. March–July.

S. *californica*—California Skullcap. Stems 1–3 dm tall; lvs oblong, 15–25 mm long, fls white, sometimes with yellow, 15–20 mm long. Dry semi-shaded places below 7000 on w. slope north of Tuolumne Co. FW, C, MCF. June–July.

The common name for S. *tuberosa* and S. *californica* comes from the skullcaplike shape of the sepals.

KEY TO THE FAMILY CRASSULACEAE (STONECROP)

1a—Tiny plants, 1–9 mm tall. *Tillaea erecta.*
1b—Plants larger. See 2.

2a—Fl stem arising from side of large cluster of fleshy lvs *Dudleya cymosa.*
2b—Fl stem an elongation of main stem. See 3.

3a—Fls dark purple. *Sedum rosea.*
3b—Fls yellow. See 4.

4a—Stem lvs the same shape as basal ones S. *lanceolatum.*
4b—Stem lvs smaller and different from basal ones. See 5.

5a—Petals separate to base. S. *spathulifolium.*
5b—Petals united one-third to one-half of length. S. *obtusatum.*

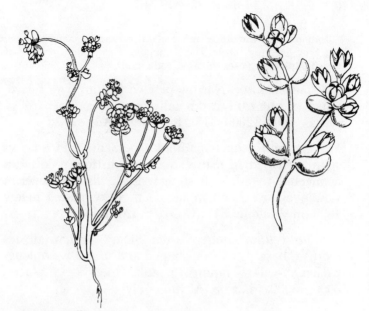

Fig. 121 *Tillaea erecta*

Genus *Tillaea*

Tillaea erecta–Pygmy Stonecrop. Fig. 121. Individual plants a slender stem with few lvs, usually in large masses appearing as yellow to reddish on rocks. Grassy, or hot open areas below 3000. FW, C. Feb–June.

Genus *Dudleya*

Dudleya cymosa–Lax or Spreading Dudleya. Pl. 9*b*. Plant a large flat basal cluster of succulent lvs, 5–10 cm long; fl stems reddish, 1–2 dm tall from the side of the leaf cluster; fls bright yellow to reddish. Rocky cliffs below 4000. FW, C. April–June.

Genus *Sedum*

Sedum rosea subsp. *integrifolium*–Rosy Sedum. Pl. 9*f*. Individual stems with many flat succulent lvs distributed up stem, 0.7–1.5 dm tall; fls dark purple. Moist places 7500–13000. MCF, MM, S, A. June–Aug.

[129]

Indians used the stems and roots as a fresh or cooked green, but they are very bitter. The distinctive Parnassius Butterfly of the subalpine area uses this as a food plant.

S. lanceolatum—Narrow-petaled Sedum. Lvs tufted, linear; fl stem 0.7–2 dm tall; fls yellow. Open rocky places, 6000–12000. MM, S, A. June–Aug.

S. spathulifolium—Spatula-leaved Sedum. Pl. 9d. Lvs spatula-shaped in many small but distinctive rosettes connected together; fl stem reddish; fls yellow on a simple cyme. Common on open rocky places below 7000 on w. slope. FW, C, MCF. April–July.

S. obtusatum—Sierra Sedum. Stem 3–16 cm tall; lvs reddish, basal lvs spoon-shaped and upper lvs oblong; fls lemon-yellow fading to pink. Open rocky places, 5000–13000. MCF, S, A. June–July.

KEY TO THE FAMILY SAXIFRAGACEAE (SAXIFRAGE)

1a—Lvs huge, umbrellalike, growing in flowing streams. *Peltiphyllum peltatum.*
1b—Lvs much smaller. See 2.

2a—Fertile stamens 10. See 3.
2b—Fertile stamens 5. See 7.

3a—Lvs and fls strongly cleft. *Lithophragma.*
3b—Lvs and fls undivided or nearly so. See 4.

4a—Lvs cylindrical. *Saxifraga tolmiei.*
4b—Lvs flat. See 5.

5a—Petals alternately of unlike size. *S. bryophora.*
5b—Petals all alike. See 6.

6a—Plants purplish, alpine. *S. aprica.*
6b—Plants green, low foothills. *S. californica.*

7a—Single fl on leafless stem. *Parnassia palustris.*
7b—Many fls on each stem. See 8.

8a—Each petal slenderly branched. *Pectiantia.*
8b—Each petal slender and unbranched. See 9.

9a—From a bulbous base. *Bolandra californica.*
9b—From a scaly stem. See 10.

10a—Petals whitish. *Heuchera micrantha.*
10b—Petals pinkish. *H. rubescens.*

Genus *Peltiphyllum*

Peltiphyllum peltatum—Umbrella Plant or Indian Rhubarb. Lf stalk stout, 3–10 dm tall; lvs 3–6 dm wide; fls white to pink. Grows characteristically only on rocks in shallow flowing streams in shade below 7000 on w. slope. PP, MCF. April–July.

Indians ate the peeled leaf stalks fresh in salads, or stewed.

Genus *Lithophragma*

Lithophragma glabrum—Rock Star. Large basal lvs, each roundish with 3 lobes, nearly leafless stem 1–3.5 dm tall, fls pinkish with 10 stamens. Dry open areas, 3500–11000 on w. slope. MCF, S. April–July.

Genus *Saxifraga*

Saxifraga tolmiei—Alpine Saxifrage. Fig. 122. Lvs densely tufted, oblong; fl stem 0.3–1.2 dm long, often reddish, petals white. Moist rocky places, 8500–12000. S, A. July–Aug.

Food plant of the Parnassius Butterfly.

S. *bryophora*—Bud Saxifrage. Fig. 124. Lvs in basal tuft, linear; fl stem slender, 0.5–2 dm, petals white with two yellow spots of unequal size on each. Moist places, 7000–11000. MCF, S, MM. July–Aug.

S. *aprica*—Sierra Saxifrage. Fig. 123. Lvs in basal tuft, purplish green, oblong; fl stalk leafless with a terminal cluster of greenish fls. Common in alpine meadows. MM, A. July–Aug.

Fig. 122 *Saxifraga tolmiei*   Fig. 123 *Saxifraga aprica*

S. californica—California Saxifrage. Lvs ovate in basal cluster, 1–5 cm long; fl stem 1–3 dm tall, petals 3–5 mm long, purplish. Common in shady places below 3000 on w. slope. FW. Feb–June.

Genus *Parnassia*

Parnassia palustris var. *californica*—California Grass of Parnassus. Fig. 125. Lvs ovate, basal, 2.5–4 cm long; stems leafless, 2.5–5 dm tall; fl single, yellowish-white, with undivided petals. Open areas of wet meadows and streams below 11000. MM. July–Oct.

Genus *Pectiantia*

Pectiantia breweri—Brewer's Mitrewort. Fig. 126. (See p. 58.) Lvs. basal; fl stems leafless, 1–3 dm tall; fls greenish with petal a distinctive slender thread with threadlike side branches appearing as a 2-sided comb. Shady places, 6000–12000. MCF. June–Aug.

Genus *Bolandra*

Bolandra californica—Sierra Bolandra. Fig. 127. (See

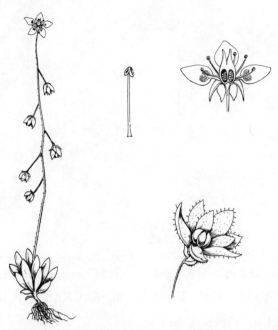

Fig. 124 *Saxifraga bryophora*

p. 110.) Base bulbous; lvs round to heart-shaped, 5–7-lobed; petals slender threadlike, greenish with purplish tips. Wet rocks, 2500–8000, Mariposa Co. and north. FW, MCF. June–July.

Genus *Heuchera*

Heuchera micrantha var. *erubescens*—Small-flowered Heuchera or Alum Root. Fig. 128. Exposed scaly rhizome; lvs 5–7 -lobed; fl stems stout, 3–7 dm tall, nearly leafless; petals slender threadlike, whitish. Shady places below 7000 on w. slope. FW, MCF. May–July.

Indians used the raw roots of this and Pink Heuchera to stop diarrhea.

H. rubescens—Pink Heuchera. Similar to *H. micrantha* except lvs sharply toothed, 3–5-lobed; petals slender, threadlike, pinkish. Shady places, 6000–12000, common. MCF, S. May–July.

[133]

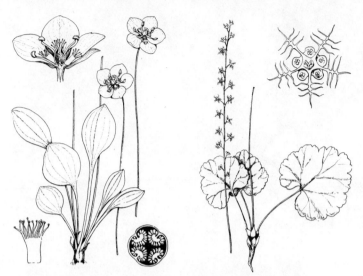

Fig. 125 *Parnassia palustris*   Fig. 126 *Pectiantia breweri*

KEY TO THE FAMILY ROSACEAE (ROSE)

1a—Lf of 3 leaflets. See 2.
1b—Lf of more than 3 leaflets. See 3.

2a—Leaflet tip 3-toothed. *Sibbaldia procumbens.*
2b—Leaflet tip many-toothed. *Fragaria platypetala.*

3a—Terminal leaflet largest. *Geum macrophyllum.*
3b—Terminal leaflet similar to others. See 4.

4a—Stamens 20. See 5.
4b—Stamens 5, 10, or 15. See 9.

5a—Styles enlarged in middle. *Potentilla pseudosericea.*
5b—Styles threadlike. See 6.

6a—Basal lvs elongate, pinnate into 5 or more leaflets. See 7.
6b—Basal lvs fingerlike (palmate). *P. gracilis.*

7a—Lvs densely white haired. *P. breweri.*
7b—Lvs green, nearly hairless. See 8.

8a—Fls white or creamy yellow. *P. glandulosa.*
8b—Fls bright yellow. *P. drummondii.*

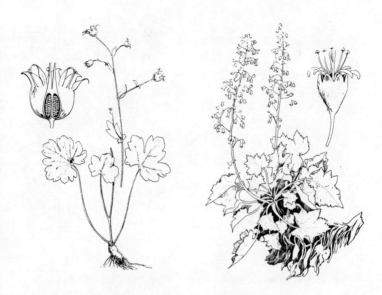

Fig. 127 *Bolandra californica*   Fig. 128 *Heuchera micrantha*

9a—Fls white (if 15 stamens see 12). See 10.
9b—Fls yellow. See 11.

10a—5–20 pairs of leaflets. *Horkelia fusca.*
10b—2–5 pairs of leaflets. *H. tridentata.*

11a—Stamens 5 or 10. See 12.
11b—Stamens 15. *Ivesia santolinoides.*

12a—Stamens 10. *I. pygmaea.*
12b—Stamens 5. See 13.

13a—Lvs densely silvery-silky. *I. muirii.*
13b—Lvs green See 14.

14a—5–10 pairs of leaflets. *I. shockleyi.*
14b—12–40 pairs of leaflets. See 15.

15a—8–18 pistils. *I. lycopodioides.*
15b—1–8 pistils, silvery. *I. gordonii.*

Genus *Sibbaldia*

Sibbaldia procumbens—Sibbaldia. Stem creeping, 1–4

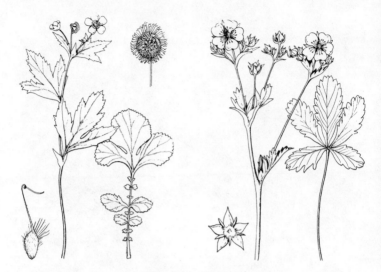

Fig. 129 *Geum macrophyllum*   Fig. 130 *Potentilla gracilis*

cm long; each lf of 3 leaflets of which each tip is 3-toothed; fls yellow. Dry rocky places, 6000–12000. MM, S, A. June–Aug.

Genus *Fragaria*

Fragaria platypetala—Broad-petaled Strawberry. Each lf of 3 leaflets; fls several, white, and later small red edible berries. Shady woods, 4000–10000 on w. slope. PP, MCF. May–June.

The lucky finder of the small red berries can be assured of a taste treat so superb that commercial strawberries seem nearly tasteless in comparison. Indians made a tea from the leaves.

Genus *Geum*

Geum macrophyllum—Large-leaved Avens. Fig. 129. Stems stout, 3–10 dm tall, bristly-hairy; lvs with large rounded terminal leaflet; fls few, yellow. MM, MCF, S. May–Aug.

Genus *Potentilla*

Potentilla pseudosericea—Strigose Cinquefoil. Lvs

Fig. 131 *Potentilla breweri*   Fig. 132 *Potentilla glandulosa*

densely hairy, in low basal cluster, pinnate with 7–11 leaflets; fls yellow, 20 stamens, style enlarged in middle. Dry places, 10500–13000, on Sierra crest and e. slope. S, A. July–Aug.

The entire *Potentilla* genus provides seeds for grouse, rosy finches, rabbits, chipmunks, and Copper Butterflies.

P. gracilis subsp. *nuttallii*—Slender Cinquefoil. Fig. 130. Lvs basal with 5–7 leaflets; stem 4–7 dm tall; fls bright yellow. Very common in moist meadows and along streams below 10000. MM. June–Aug.

P. breweri—Brewer's Cinquefoil. Fig. 131. (See p. 58.) Lvs basal, 2–5 lance oblong leaflets with dense white hairs; fls yellow. 4500–12000 on crest and e. slope. MM, S. June–Aug.

P. drummondii—Drummond's Cinquefoil. (See p. 22.) Similar to *P. breweri*, but leaflets deeply cleft and dark green, almost hairless; fls yellow. Common in wet places, 6000–12000. MM, MCF, S. July–Aug.

P. glandulosa—Sticky Cinquefoil. Fig. 132. Lvs basal,

[137]

Fig. 133 *Ivesia santolinoides*   Fig. 134 *Ivesia gordonii*

pinnate with 5–9 leaflets; stems 3–8 dm tall; stem and lvs slightly sticky; fls white or creamy yellow. Common in moist meadows and streams below 9000. MM. June–Aug.

Genus *Horkelia*

Horkelia fusca—Dusky Horkelia. Lvs basal, 2–3.5 dm long with 5–10 pairs of bright green leaflets; stems 1–5 dm tall; fls white. Shaded woods, 3500–8000, Yosemite north. MM. July–Aug.

The genus was named for J. Horkel, a German physiologist.

H. tridentata—Three-toothed Horkelia. Lvs with each leaflet tip 3-toothed; stem purplish with silky hairs; fls white. Shaded woods, 2000–6500 on w. slope. MCF. May–July.

Genus *Ivesia*

The genus was named for Lt. E. Ives, a leader of a Pacific Railroad Survey.

Ivesia santolinoides—Mouse-tail Ivesia. Fig. 133. Lvs in

[138]

crowded basal rosette, densely silvery-silky, which consists of numerous tiny leaflets; fls white. Widespread on dry ridges, 5000–12000, southern Sierra. PJ, MCF. June–Aug.

I. pygmaea—Dwarf Ivesia. Lvs pinnate, in crowded basal cluster, each lf with 10–20 pairs of tiny leaflets, also minutely hairy and sticky; fls light yellow, 10 stamens. Alpine slopes of Tulare and Fresno cos. 9500–13000. A. July–Aug.

I. muirii—Muir's Ivesia. Lvs many, basal, each pinnate lf with 25–40 pairs of tiny leaflets with silvery-silky hairs; fls yellow in dense heads, 5 stamens per fl. Alpine slopes, 9500–12000. A. July–Aug.

Named for John Muir who knew the alpine plants as his friends.

I. shockleyi—Shockley's Ivesia. Stems 0.3–1 dm tall; each lf with 7–10 pairs of leaflets covered with dense hairs. Gravelly meadows 9000–13000, Tioga Pass south. S, A. July–Aug.

I. lycopodioides—Club Moss Ivesia. Pl. 9c. Lvs hairless in dense clusters with 12–40 leaflets; fls bright yellow with 8–18 pistils. Dry gravelly places in alpine meadows, 10000–13000. MM, S, A. July–Aug.

I. gordonii—Gordon's Ivesia. Fig. 134. Plant low to ground; lvs slightly hairy and sticky, 10–25 pairs of leaflets; fls yellow. Dry slopes, 7500–13000. MM, S, A. July–Aug.

Indians dug the root just before seeds matured and made a tea for heart trouble.

KEY TO THE FAMILY LEGUMINOSAE (PEA)

1a—Leaflets palmate (fiingerlike), 3–10. See 2.
1b—Leaflets pinnate (featherlike). See 5.

2a—Leaflets 4–10. *Lupinus.*
2b Leaflets 3. See 3.

3a—Fls in heads. *Trifolium.*
3b—Fls loosely arranged spikes. See 4.

4a—Plants tall, 1–2 m. *Melilotus.*
4b—Plants low less than 9 dm. *Medicago.*

5a—End of lf a tendril. See 6.
5b—End of lf without tendril. See 7.

6a—Banner petal upright. *Lathyrus.*
6b—Banner petal close to keel. *Vicia.*

7a—Fls in umbels or single. *Lotus.*
7b—Fls in raceme. *Astragalus.*

Key to the Genus *Lupinus*

1a—Lvs hairless above. See 2.
1b—Lvs hairy above. See 4.

2a—Fls white, tinted rose. *L. densiflorus.*
2b—Fls blue-purple. See 3.

3a—10–17 leaflets per lf. *L. polyphyllus.*
3b—7–9 leaflets per lf. *L. latifolius.*

4a—Fls bright yellow and pink. *L. stiversii.*
4b—Fls variously purple, blue to whitish. See 5.

5a—Plants less than 2 dm tall. See 6.
5b—Plants more than 2 dm tall. See 10.

6a—Small annual, no old dead stems at stem base, fls in obvious
    whorls. See 7.
6b—Perennials, old dead stems at stem base, fls not in whorls.
    See 8.

```
1 millimeter
10 millimeters = 1 centimeter = 13/32 inch
10 centimeters = 1 decimeter = ca. 4 inches
10 decimeters = 1 meter = 3.3 feet
```

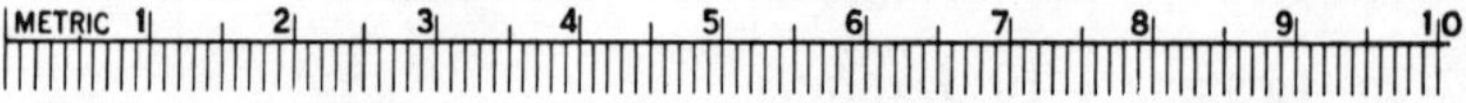

Fig. 135 Metric scale 1:1

7a—Fls rich blue with a white or yellow spot on banner. *L. nanus.*
7b—Fls deep blue with a white banner spot having purple dots. *L. micranthus.*

8a—No hairs along top edge of keel petal. *L. lepidus.*
8b—Hairs along top edge of keel petal. See 9.

9a—Lvs silvery-silky. *L. breweri.*
9b—Lvs slightly hairy, not silvery. *L. hypolasius.*

10a—Hairs along top edge of keel petal. See 11.
10b—No hairs on top edge of keel petal. See 13.

11a—Fls purple to blue with pale white center. *L. lepidus* var. *confertus.*
11b—Fls purplish to pale blue, central yellow spot. See 12.

12a—Subalpine forest or alpine. *L. covillei.*
12b—Red fir forest or lower. *L. grayi.*

13a—Fl pale blue with yellow spot. *L. benthamii.*
13b—Fl whitish to purplish, no yellow spot. See 14.

14a—Fls 12–16 mm long. *L. albicaulis.*
14b—Fls 10-12 mm long. *L. andersonii.*

The genus name comes from the Latin *lupus* = wolf, because it was thought these plants robbed the soil. Actually certain bacteria in the root nodules convert gaseous nitrogen into organic forms for plant use, and so enrich the soil. Redness of the nodules is due to a hemoglobinlike compound that resembles that found in human blood. Some of the many lupines contain various alkaloids that are poisonous to man, cattle, and sheep. The seeds are edible to various species of birds, squirrels, chipmunks, and deer. Many butterfly caterpillars depend on plants of this genus for food, including the Blues and Hairstreaks. Stem galls are caused by eggs laid by the Lupine Stem Gall Wasp.

Lupinus densiflorus—Dense-flowered Lupine. Pl. 9*e*. Stem often hollow, 2–4 dm tall; lvs hairless above, fls

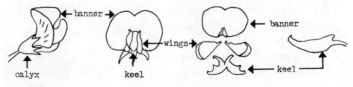

Fig. 136

white in whorls, tinted rose. Open areas below 6000 on w. slope. FW, C. April–May.

L. *polyphyllus*–Large-leaved Lupine. Stem 5–15 dm tall; lf tops hairless, 10–17 leaflets per lf; fls blue, purple, or reddish. Wet places, 4000–8500. PP, MCF. May–July.

L. *latifolius*–Broad-leaved Lupine. Pl. 10a. Stem 3–12 dm tall; lf tops hairless and basal lvs often dry by flowering time, 7–9 leaflets per lf; fls blue or purple, occasionally tinted pink. Common in open woods below 7000. PP, MCF. April–July.

L. *stiversii*–Stiver's Lupine. Pl. 10b. Stems 1–4.5 dm tall; fls multicolored with a yellow banner, rose-pink. wings and white keel. Sandy open places below 6000 on w. slope. MCF. April–July.

L. *nanus* subsp. *latifolius*–Douglas's Lupine. (See p. 54.) Annual. Plants usually in masses 1–5 dm tall; fls in distinct whorls, a rich blue with a white or yellowish spot on the banner. Open grassy fields below 4000 on w. slope. FW, C. April–May.

L. *micranthus*–Tiny-flowered Lupine. Plants small, found near base of grasses, less than 1 dm tall; fls tiny, dark blue with a white spot on banner having purple dots, 6–8 mm long. Open places below 5000 on w. slope. FW, C. March–June.

L. *lepidus* var. *lyallii*–Lyall's Lipine. (See p. 50.) Plant low; stems prostrate, 5–12 cm tall; fls pale blue. Common in open areas above 8000. *L. lepidus* var. *confertus*. Stems stout, 2–3.5 dm tall; lvs densely white-silky; fls purple to blue with white center. Common below 8000. MCF, MM. June–Aug.

L. *breweri*–Brewer's Lupine. (See p. 58.) Plant low, prostrate or matted; lvs silvery-gray; fls blue-violet with white or yellow center, hairs on top of keel. Very common on dry slopes above 4000. MCF. June–Aug.

L. hypolasius–Farewell Gap Lupine. Plant loosely matted, slightly hairy; fls purple or blue, keel hairy. Rocky open places, 9500–11000, Mono Pass to Mineral King. S, A. July–Aug.

Named for the place where it was discovered near Mineral King.

L. covillei–Coville's Lupine. (See p. 93.) Stems 2–8 dm tall, loosely silky haired; fls blue with large yellowish center spot. 8500–10000, Tuolumne Meadows and south. S, A. July–Sept.

L. grayi–Gray's Lupine. Stems several, 2–3.5 dm tall; densely gray-haired; fls purplish-blue, 12–14 mm long with yellow center. Dry slopes below 8000 on w. slope, frequent in Yosemite. MCF. May–July.

Named for Asa Gray (1810–1888), prominent botanist at Harvard, who named many of the newly discovered plants sent to him by early explorers of the West.

L. benthamii–Bentham's Lupine. Stem erect, 3–6 dm tall; fls pale blue with yellow spot in elongated spikes. Very frequent along roadsides, openings below 4000 on w. slope. FW, C. March–June.

Named for George Bentham, a prominent botanist at Kew in England, who worked on a world plant classification system during the time of Charles Darwin.

L. albicaulis–Sickle-keeled Lupine. Stem 4–9 dm tall; lvs green slightly hairy; fls 12–16 mm long, whitish to purple fading brown, no hairs on top edge of keel, which is sickle-shaped. Dry open areas below 8500. PP, MCF. May–Aug.

L. andersonii–Anderson's Lupine. Similar to *L. albicaulis* except fls 10–12 mm long, blue or yellowish white, keel hairless. Dry pine woods, 4000–8500, Yosemite north. PP. June–Sept.

Key to the Genus *Trifolium* (Clover)

1a—Prominent bract surrounding and below all fls in the head. See 2.
1b—No bract below fls. See 5.

2a—Bract flat. See 3.
2b—Bract bowl-shaped. See 4.

3a—Plant sticky and hairy. *T. obtusiflorum.*
3b—Plant not sticky and few haired. *T. monanthum.*

4a—Lobes of bract undivided. *T. microcephalum.*
4b—Lobes of bract toothed. *T. cyathiferum.*

5a—Plant long haired. *T. breweri.*
5b—Plant hairless or nearly so. *T. repens.*

The clover genus contains many species. Indians ate the greens after boiling in salt water, but overeating results in a serious stomach bloat. A number of birds depend on the foliage and seeds, as do squirrels and deer. It is also a food source for the Sulphur, Blue, and Dusky-Wing butterflies.

Trifolium obtusiflorum—Creek or Clammy Clover. Lvs soft, hairy, clammy to touch, lf edges saw-toothed; fls pale with central dark spot, in large heads. Moist places below 5000. PP, MCF. April–June.

T. monanthum—Carpet Clover. Fig. 137. Stems 1–10 cm long, hairless to slightly hairy; plants usually in a large matted carpet with many cream fls with purple-tipped keels. Common, wet meadows, 5000–12000. MCF, MM, S. June–Aug.

T. microcephalum—Small-headed Clover. Stems slender, 2–4 dm long, hairy; fls rose to white in small heads. Open grassy places below 8500 on w. slope. MCF, MM. April–Aug.

T. cyathiferum—Bowl Clover. Plant hairless, with conspicuous whitish bowl-like bract below fl head; fls pink or paler. Moist places below 8000. MCF, MM. May–Aug.

T. breweri—Brewer's Clover. Fig. 138. (See p. 58.)

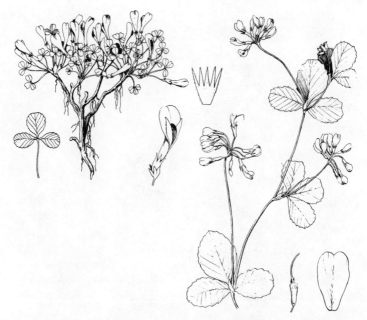

Fig. 137 *Trifolium monanthum*   Fig. 138 *Trifolium brewerii*

Stems 1–3 dm long; leaflets obovate with notched tip, long haired; fls rose to cream. Shaded woods below 6500 on w. slope. PP, MCF. May–Aug.

T. repens—White Clover. Stems creeping, hairless; fls white to pale pink in globelike heads. FW, MCF, MM. Most months.

Frequently used in lawns or naturalized in moist meadows. Introduced from Europe.

Genus *Melilotus*

Melilotus albus—Sweet Clover. Fig. 139. Stems very tall, 1–2 m, much-branched; fls white or yellow. Frequent in disturbed places and along roads. FW, C, MCF, MM. May–Sept.

Introduced from Europe. Sweet Clover emits a strong sweet odor on warm days. Sometimes the yellow-flowered plants are considered a separate species, although they are found together with the white.

[145]

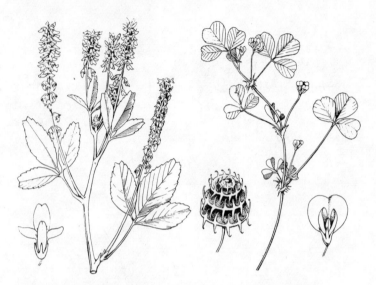

Fig. 139 *Melilotus albus*   Fig. 140 *Medicago hispida*

Key to the Genus *Medicago* (Medick)

1a—Fls blue. *Medicago sativa.*
1b—Fls yellow. *M. hispida.*

Medicago sativa—Alfalfa. Stems erect 4–9 dm tall; fls blue-violet, seed pods coiled but not spiny. FW, MM. All year.

Cultivated and often naturalized. The generic name is from the Greek word *medice* = alfalfa, which originally came from Medea, Greece. Important livestock food.

M. hispida—Bur Clover. Fig. 140. Plant low, somewhat prostrate; fls yellow with spiny coiled seed pods. Very widespread. FW, MM. All year.

Introduced from Europe.

Key to the Genus *Lathyrus* (Sweet Pea)

1a—Fls yellowish. *Lathyrus sulphureus.*
1b—Fls purplish to white. See 2.

2a—Fls pale blue purple, tendril usually lacking. *L. nevadensis.*
2b—Fls bright red purple or sometimes white, tendril present. *L. latifolius.*

[146]

The caterpillar of the various blue butterflies use the sweet pea for food.

Lathyrus sulphureus—Brewer's Pea or Sulphur Pea. See p. 58.) Stems sprawling to 3 m; fls tan to yellowish with some purple or orange tint. Dry semi-shaded areas below 8000 on w. slope. FW, C, MCF. April–July.

L. *nevadensis*—Sierra Nevada Pea. Stems short, 1.5–4 dm long; each lf with 4–8 leaflets with terminal position a poorly developed tendril or a linear point; fls dark blue-reddish with a white keel. Dry shady woods, frequent below 7000 on w. slope. PP. April–July.

L. *latifolius*—Everlasting Pea. Pl. 10c. Stems long, sprawling or climbing, with winged margins, well-developed tendrils; fls all bright red-purple or white. Common about old mining towns. FW, MM. May–July.

Introduced from Europe.

Genus *Vicia*

Vicia americana—American Vetch. Fig. 141. Stem trailing or climbing, 6–12 dm long; fls many in a raceme, purplish, aging blue. Frequent in open places below 5000. FW, C, MCF, MM. April–July.

Key to the Genus *Lotus* (Bird's Foot Trefoil or Deer Vetch)

1a—Fls pinkish turning red. L. *micranthus*.
1b—Fls with some yellow. See 2.

2a—In wet springy places. L. *oblongifolius*.
2b—On dry flats or slopes. See 3.

3a—Fls greenish yellow. L. *crassifolius*.
3b—Fls yellow. See 4.

4a—Plants densely silvery-haired. L. *argophyllus*.
4b—Plants slightly haired. L. *nevadensis*.

Important as foliage for cattle; seeds are food for doves, quail, rabbits, pocket mice, and deer.

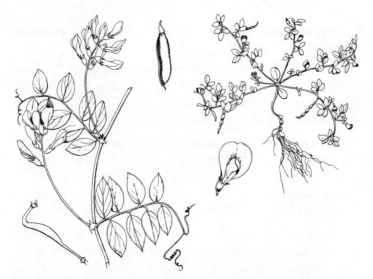

Fig. 141 *Vicia americana* Fig. 142 *Lotus micranthus*

Lotus micranthus—Small-flowered Lotus. Fig. 142. Stems slender, 1–3 dm tall, mostly hairless; fl single, pinkish or orangish turning red with age. Open areas below 5000 on w. slope. FW, C, MCF. March–May.

L. oblongifolius—Narrow-leaved Lotus. Pl. 10*d*. Stems 2–5 dm tall; each lf with 7–11 leaflets; fls in umbel, distinctive yellow banner and wings with a white keel. Common in wet springy places below 9000. MM, MCF. June–Aug.

L. crassifolius—Broad-leaved Lotus. Stems stout 4–12 dm tall, hairless or minutely haired; fls greenish yellow with some purplish red, pods 3.5–6.5 cm long. Dry flats below 8000 on w. slope. MCF. May–Aug.

L. argophyllus—Silver-leaved Lotus. Stem sprawling and many-branched, 2–10 dm long, densely silvery haired; fls yellow with banner brown or purple in age. Dry slopes below 5000. FW, C. April–July.

L. nevadensis—Sierra Nevada Lotus. Stems many, sprawling, wiry, mostly hairless; fls yellow or tinted

[148]

red; pods short, 6 mm long. Dry sandy places below 8500 on w. slope. MCF. May–Aug.

Key to the Genus *Astragalus*
(Locoweed or Rattleweed)

1a—Leaflets spine-tipped. *A. kentrophyta.*
1b—Leaflets not spine-tipped. See 2.

2a—Pods densely white hairy. See 3.
2b—Pods hairless or nearly so. See 4.

3a—Fls whitish or lilac tinged. *A. austinae.*
3b—Fls pink-purple, drying crimson. *A. purshii.*

4a—Pod long-curved, sausage-shaped. *A. bolanderi.*
4b—Pod variously ovoid. See 5.

5a—Pod beak (tip) not curved. See 6.
5b—Pod beak strongly curved. *A. lentiginosus.*

6a—Pod balloonlike, nearly beakless. *A. whitneyi.*
6b—Pod balloonlike, beak slightly inflated. *A. platytropis.*

Most species in this large genus, found throughout the west, are poisonous to man and cattle due to uptake of selenium or arsenic from the soil. The common name is from the Spanish word *loco* = crazy. Horses and cattle become dull and unsteady as though the brain had ceased to function after eating *Astragalus,* and eventually they will die. On the other hand, this genus provides food for marmots, mice, and the Blues, and Hair Streak butterflies.

Astragalus kentrophyta—Alpine Spring Locoweed. Fig. 143. Plant cushionlike; lvs narrow, phloxlike, greenish or white; fls pink-purple with pale wing tips, pod compressed ellipsoid. 9000–11000. S. June–Sept.

A. austinae—Austin's Locoweed. Dwarf plant, lvs gray; fls whitish or tinted blue; pod small, oblong, hairy. Peaks north of Ebbets Pass, 9000–11000. S, A. June–Aug.

Named for Mrs. Rebecca Austin, an early amateur botanist who explored the northern Sierra.

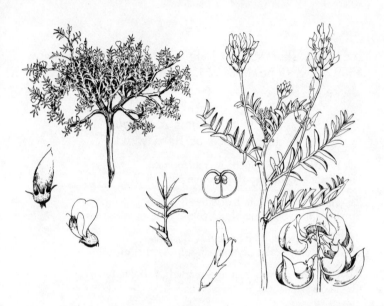

Fig. 143 *Astragalus kentrophyta*   Fig. 144 *Astragalus bolanderi*

A. *purshii*—Pursh's Wooly Pod or Sheep Pod. Dwarf plant; lvs white-haired; fls pink-purple drying crimson; pods obliquely ovoid with dense shaggy hair. Below 11000 on e. slope. PJ, MCF, S. May–Aug.

A. *bolanderi*—Bolander's Locoweed. (See p. 110.) Fig. 144. Stems nearly hairless, 1.5–4.5 dm tall; fls whitish tinted pink; pod curved sausagelike, 1–3 cm long, hairless. Dry meadows and flats, 5000–10000, common. MM, MCF. June–Aug.

A. *lentiginosus*—Mottled Locoweed. Plant erect or low, highly variable; fls whitish to pinkish or more often purple; pods strongly inflated, subglobose with inflated beak strongly curved over seed pod. Widespread, most communities. May–Aug.

A. *whitneyi*—Whitney's Locoweed. Pl. 10e. Stems sprawling, dwarfed at higher elevations, .3–2.5 dm long; fls purple with white wings, large inflated yellowish pods mottled purple. Rocky places, 7000–12000. S, A. May–Sept.

[150]

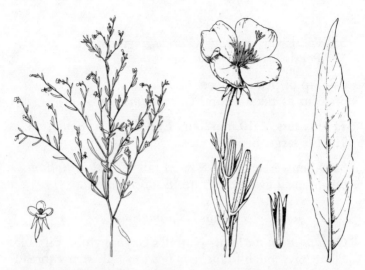

Fig. 145 *Gayophytum nuttallii*   Fig. 146 *Oenothera hookeri*

Named for Josiah D. Whitney, who explored the Sierra as a geologist in the 1860s, and who later became head of the U.S. Geological Survey. Mt. Whitney, 14,494 ft., the highest Sierra peak is also named for him.

A. platytropis—Broad-keeled Locoweed. Dwarf plant, tufted, silvery haired, fls yellowish, tinted leaden purple; pod mottled, inflated including beak. Alpine areas mostly on volcanic soil. S, A. July–Aug.

KEY TO THE FAMILY ONAGRACEAE
(EVENING PRIMROSE)

1a—Seeds without a tuft of hairs at one end. See 2.
1b—Seeds with tuft of hairs at one end (open oldest seed pod for best results). See 7.

2a—Fls mostly 2 mm long, tiny. *Gayophytum nuttallii.*
2b—Fls longer than 5 mm. See 3.

3a—Fls yellow. *Oenothera hookeri.*
3b—Fls pink to white. See 4.

4a—Fls white. *Oenothera caespitosa.*
4b—Fls pink to dark rose-red. See 5.

[151]

5a—Petals very narrow. *Clarkia unguiculata.*
5b—Petals broad to base. See 6.

6a—Tip of petal 2-lobed. *C. biloba.*
6b—Tip of petal entire. *C. williamsonii.*

7a—Fls tiny, 2–10 mm long. *Epilobium paniculatum.*
7b—Fls large. See 8.

8a—Stems erect, ½ to 2½ m tall. *E. angustifolium.*
8b—Stems low or prostrate, *E. obcordatum.*

Genus *Gayophytum*

Gayophytum nuttallii—Nuttall's Gayophytum. Fig. 145. Plant low, much-branched, 1–2 dm tall; stems thread-like; fls white drying pink, ca. 2 mm long. Frequent on open flats or near springs below 12000. Most communities. May–Aug.

Genus *Oenothera*

Oenothera hookeri—Hooker's Evening Primrose. Fig. 146. Stem tall, nearly unbranched, 1.5–2.5 m high; fls with large yellow petals, 3–4.5 cm long. Moist seeps below 6000 on w. and e. slopes. FW, C, MCF, PJ, SS. June–Oct.

Named for Sir Joseph Hooker, director of Royal Botanic Gardens, Kew, and the co-author with George Bentham of a generic flora of the world.

O. caespitosa—Low Evening Primrose. Plant is low cluster of linear lvs; fls many, very large, white, which open in late afternoon and wilt next morning, 2.5–4 cm across each 4-petaled fl. Common on sandy flats along e. slope. SS, PJ. May–July.

Genus *Clarkia*

The genus *Clarkia* is named for Captain William Clark of the Lewis and Clark expedition.

Clarkia unguiculata—Elegant Clarkia. Fig. 147. Stems

Fig. 147 *Clarkia unguiculata*   Fig. 148 *Epilobium paniculatum*

simple, 2–11 dm tall; lvs oblong; fls with buds nodding, petals quite narrow, 6–12 mm long, outer tip triangular, pinkish often red at base. Dry open areas below 5000 on w. slope. FW, C. May–July.

C. biloba—Two-lobed Clarkia. Pl. 10*f*. Stems simple, 3–10 dm tall; lvs linear; fls with buds nodding, petals pink with each tip bilobed. Open grassy places below 5000 on w. slope. FW, YPF. May–July.

C. williamsonii—Williamson's Clarkia. Stem simple, 2–10 dm tall; lvs linear; fls with buds erect, petals broad 1–3 cm, lavender with both white and purple spot in center of each petal. Dry open grassy places below 6000 on w. slope. FW, C. May–Aug.

C. biloba and *C. williamsonii* are frequently found together.

Genus *Epilobium*

Epilobium paniculatum—Panicled Willow Herb. Fig.

[153]

Fig. 149 *Epilobium angustifolium*

148. Stems erect, 1–8 dm tall; fls small, pinkish, 2–10 mm long. Often in masses near damp places below 10000, common. Most communities. June–Aug.

E. angustifolium—Fireweed. Fig. 149. Stems single ½ to 2½ m tall; fls many, rose-purple, in a terminal spike. Frequent below 11000. FW, MCF, MM, S, A. July–Sept.

Indians ate the young tender leaves and stems as greens, or peeled the stem for the pith. Although somewhat bitter this plant was an important early spring source of vitamin C and pro-vitamin A. Great masses of this species appear on sites disturbed by fire the previous year. It is food for chipmunks and deer.

E. obcordatum—Rock Fringe. Stems low, matted along boulder bases; fls rose-purple, 1–2 cm broad. Open ridges 7000–13000. S, A. July–Sept.

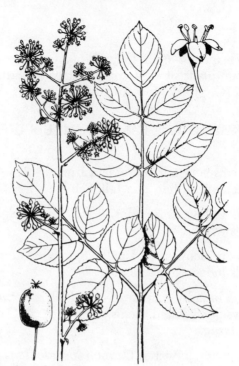

Fig. 150 *Aralia californica*

FAMILY ARISTOLOCHIACEAE (BIRTHWORT)

Asarum hartwegii—Hartweg's Ginger. Pl. 11*a*. Fls dark brownish-purple, hidden below the few large heart-shaped lvs mottled with white. In shady woods below 7000 on w. slope. FW, MCF. May–July.

Named for Theodor Karl Hartweg who was sent by the English to explore California during the early 1800s. George Bentham later published an account of Hartweg's discoveries. This species has been used as a substitute for commercial ginger. Flies, attracted by the fetid odor of the flower, pollinate this plant.

FAMILY ARALIACEAE (GINSENG)

Genus *Aralia*

Aralia californica—Californa Spikenard or Elk Clover. Fig. 150. Stems very tall, 1–3 m; each lf is 3-sectioned into 3–5 leaflets, 3–6 dm long; fls many, in umbels. A conspicuous plant of cool shaded stream bottoms below 7000. MCF, FW. June–Aug.

KEY TO THE FAMILY UMBELLIFERAE
(CARROT)

1a—Stems very tall, more than 1 m. See 2.
1b—Stems less than 1 m tall. See 5.

2a—Fls yellow, anise odor. *Foeniculum vulgare*.
2b—Fls white. See 3.

3a—Fls in dense round balls. *Sphenosciadium*.
3b—Fls in loose umbelet. See 4.

4a—Lvs broadly pinnate, 3-lobed, *Heracleum lanatum*.
4b—Lvs finely lobed, stems purple dotted. *Conium maculatum*.

5a—Growing in water. *Oxypolis occidentalis*.
5b—Land plants. See 6.

6a—Plants mostly 6–10 dm tall. See 7.
6b—Plants prostrate to 5 dm tall. See 10.

7a—3–5 fls per umbelet. See 8.
7b—Many fls per umbelet. See 9.

8a—Seeds elongate, ribs not bristly. *Osmorhiza occidentalis*.
8b—Seeds with bristly ribs. *O. chilensis*.

9a—Basal lvs with 3–5 linear pinnae. *Perideridia parishii*.
9b—Basal lvs with 6–9 pinnae which are further divided. *P. bolanderi*.

10a—Fls white in small rounded head. *Cymopterus*.
10b—Fls in umbel. See 11.

11a—Lvs not divided into distinct leaflets. *Podistera nevadensis*.
11b—Lvs divided into leaflets. See 12.

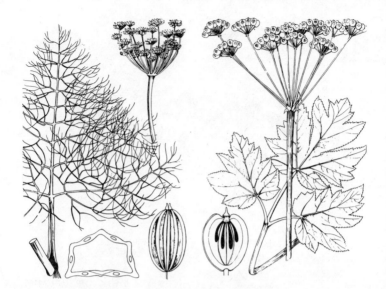

Fig. 151 *Foeniculum vulgare*   Fig. 152 *Heracleum lanatum*

12a—Winged margins of seed hairy. *Oreonana clementis.*

12b—Winged margins of seed smooth. See 13.

13a—No wings on seed, edges smooth. *Ligusticum.*
13b—Seeds with wings. See 14.

14a—Few or 2 wings per seed. *Lomatium nudicaule.*
14b—Many wings per seed. *Pteryxia terebinthina.*

Genus *Foeniculum*

Foeniculum vulgare—Sweet Fennel. Fig. 151. Plant in clumps, 1–2 m tall; lvs thinly divided into threads, anise odor (licorice); fls yellow. Common in disturbed places. FW, MCF. Most of the year.

Introduced from Europe. The leaf stalks can be eaten or cooked. It is the food plant of the lovely Anise Swallowtail Butterfly.

Genus *Sphenosciadium*

Sphenosciadium   capitellatum—Ranger's   Button   or

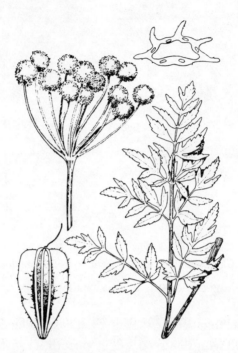

Fig. 153 *Spenosciadium capitellatum*

White Head's. Pl. 11*b*. Fig. 153. Stem tall, 1–1½ m; fls tiny white balls in umbel. Common in wet places below 12000. MM, MCF, S. July–Aug.

Genus *Heracleum*

Heracleum lanatum—Cow Parsnip. Fig. 152. Stems stout, 1–3 m tall, surface somewhat wooly; lvs with 3 large leaflets, 3–5 dm long; fls white. Frequent in moist meadows below 9000. MM. April–July.

Indians cooked the first tender shoots in the spring, like asparagus. They used the cooked roots to relieve stomach gas or to treat epilepsy. During the Sun Dance Ceremony part of a stalk was always placed on the altar. This is a food plant of the Anise Swallowtail Butterfly. Various deadly poisonous plants not described in this book closely resemble the Cow Parsnip.

[158]

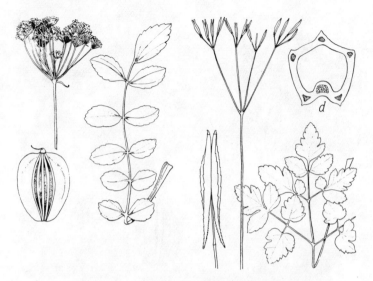

Fig. 154 *Oxypolis occidentalis*   Fig. 155 *Osmorhiza chilensis*

Genus *Conium*

Conium maculatum—Poison Hemlock. Stems 1–3 m tall with purple dots; leaflets finely divided; fls white. Common in disturbed places below 5000. FW, C, MCF. April–Sept.

Introduced from Europe. Reputed to be the plant from which the poison was obtained to execute Socrates.

Genus *Oxypolis*

Oxypolis occidentalis—Western Oxypolis or Cow Bane. Fig. 154. Stem 6–10 dm tall; fls white. Grows in wet places or damp open slopes, 4000–8500, widespread. MCF. July–Aug.

The common name suggests that it is poisonous to cattle.

Genus *Osmorhiza*

Osmorhiza occidentalis—Western Sweet Cicely. Stems slender, widely branched, 6–10 dm tall; lvs mostly at

[159]

Fig. 156 *Orenana clementis*   Fig. 157 *Ligusticum grayi*

base; fls few, becoming long slender smooth seeds.
Shady woods below 8500. FW, MCF. May–July.

Indians used the seeds for seasoning, and the roots for tea to
cure colds or as a physic.

O. chilensis—Mountain Sweet Cicely. Fig. 155. Similar to *O. occidentalis* except seeds with bristly ribs.

Genus *Perideridia*

Perideridia parishii—Parish's Yampah. Pl. 11*d*. Lvs bas-
sal, pinnate with 3 narrow pinnae or 2 pair of pinnae;
stems mostly leafless, 5–10 dm tall; fls small, white, in
umbel. Meadows, 5000 and higher. MM. June–Aug.

Indians ate the mild, nutty-flavored roots raw or baked and
stored them for winter use. It was an important Indian food
throughout the west.

P. bolanderi—Bolander's Yampah or Olaski. Lvs basal, bipinnate, 3–4 pair of linear primary pinnae, each
with many secondary linear divisions; stem leafless, 5–

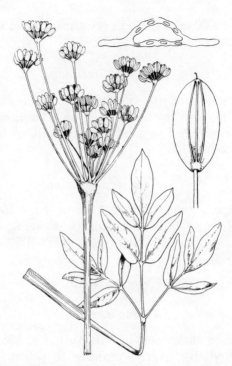

Fig. 158 *Lomatium nudicaule*

9 dm tall; fls small, white, in umbel. Meadows, 7000 and lower. FW, MCF, MM. June–Aug.

The Miwok Indians ate the Yampah; *Olaski* is the Miwok name.

Genus *Cymopterus*

Cymopterus cinerarius–Gray's Cymopterus. Pl. 11c. (See p. 143.) Plant small, few-leaved, low; fls white in a rounded head; seeds rosy. Open loose soil, 9000–11500. S, A. June–July.

Genus *Podistera*

Podistera nevadensis–Sierra Podistera. Plant cushion-like; lvs not divided into distinct leaflets; fls yellowish.

10000–13000, along Sierra crest from Mammoth to Tahoe. A. June–Sept.

Genus *Oreonana*

Oreonana clementis—Clemen's mountain Parsley. Fig. 156. Plant low; few lacy lvs; fls in a ball; seed margins hairy. Restricted to sandy alpine zone of upper Kern basin, 8000–13000. A. July–Aug.

Genus *Ligusticum*

Ligusticum grayi—Gray's Lovage. Fig. 157. (See p. 143.) Stems 1–5 dm tall, hairless; fls white to pinkish; seeds smooth. Meadow areas, 4000–10500, common. MM. June–Sept.

Indians ate the sweet roots and stems.

Genus *Lomatium*

Lomatium nudicaule—Biscuit Root. Fig. 158. Plant low to ground; lvs large, bipinnate; fls yellow; seeds distinctive, large, winged. Open areas below 7000. FW, C, MCF. April–June.

An important Indian food throughout the West. The roots were dug at a specific time and the first feast was called the "Root Feast," similar to our present Thanksgiving Dinner. *Lomatium* was "Big Medicine," too, as this genus of plants provided tea for colds, oil from roots for treating glaucoma and horse distemper, and oil for tanning. Many species occur in the West.

Genus *Pteryxia*

Pteryxia terebinthina—Terebinth Pteryxia. Stem 1–5 dm tall; lvs gray-green; fls yellow; seeds with many flattened wings. Dry brushy slopes below 10000. FW, C, MCF. May–June.

Food plant of the Indra Swallowtail Butterfly.

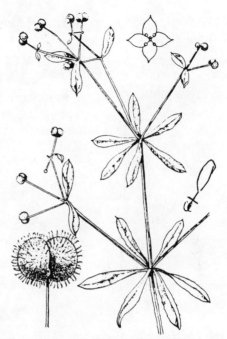

Fig. 159 *Galium aparine*

FAMILY RUBIACEAE (MADDER)

Genus *Galium*

Galium aparine—Bedstraw. Fig. 159. Stems slender, rambling, weakly 4-angled, roughly hairy; lvs linear in whorl around stem; fls small, white, usually 2 round spiny seeds per fl. Common, semi-shaded woods below 7500. FW, C, MCF. March–July.

Indians used the roots of some *Galiums* to make a red dye.

KEY TO THE FAMILY VALERIANACEAE (VALERIAN)

1a—Plants perennial, stout stems. *Valeriana*.
1b—Plants annual, stems slender. *Plectritis*.

[163]

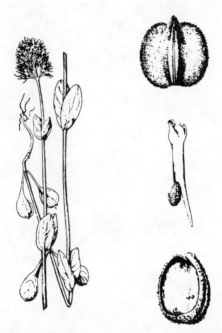

Fig. 160 *Plectritis ciliosa*

Genus *Valeriana*

Valeriana capitata subsp. *californica*—California Valerian. Stem 2–6 dm tall from a stout rhizome; lvs mostly basal; fls white to pinkish. Common in semi-moist meadows, 5000–10000. MM. July Sept.

Genus *Plectritis*

Plectritis ciliosa—Long-spurred Plectritis. Fig. 160. Plant is slender herb, 1–4 dm tall; lvs opposite, oblong; fls many, pink, with slender spur in terminal cone-shaped mass. Common in grassy places below 4000 on w. slope. FW, C. March–May.

FAMILY CUCURBITACEAE (CUCUMBER)
Genus *Marah*

Marah watsonii—Taw Man Root. Stems long, trailing,

[164]

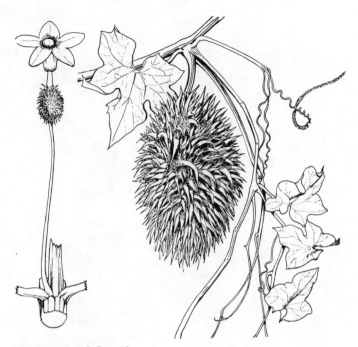

Fig. 161 *Marah horridus*

3–7 m; lvs roundish with 5 lobes, tendrils and fl branches arising from main stem; fls greenish-yellow and of spearate sexes; fruits large spiny, rounded. Frequent below 3000, Tuolumne Co. and north. *M. horridus* (fig. 161) replaces it to the south of Tuolumne Co. FW, C. March–May.

Indians roasted the large seeds and ate them as a treatment for kidney troubles. The underground root is gigantic and resembles the torso of a man.

FAMILY CAMPANULACEAE
(BELLFLOWER)

Campanula prenanthoides—California Harebell. Fig. 162. Plant is slender branched herb, 2–8 dm tall; lvs oblong; fls bright blue, bowl-shaped, in clusters of 2–5.

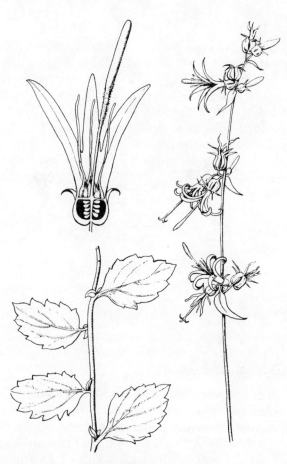

Fig. 162 *Campanula prenanthoides*

Dry shaded woods below 7000, frequent in western
Yosemite and north. MCF. June–Sept.

FAMILY COMPOSITAE (SUNFLOWER)

Compositae is one of the largest plant families and so
it is divided into subsections called tribes. Examination
of a sunflower will show that it is composed of many
small flowers grouped on a single receptacle. These
small flowers are of two types—ray flowers and disc
flowers. Rapid identification is possible if you learn the

distinction between these two flower types, and also the other sunflower parts illustrated here. When a plant is to be identified, carefully study the flowers and parts of the plant, and first go to the Master Key to the Tribes, and from there to the individual tribe key. You will see that all the tribe keys are based on the various possible combinations of a sunflower head. Shortly you should be able to recognize which tribe a flower belongs to immediately and be able to go directly to the individual tribe key.

MASTER KEY TO THE TRIBES OF SUNFLOWERS

1a—Plants spiny, fls all disc. *Cynareae.*
1b—Plants without spines. See 2.

2a—Both ray and disc fls in one fl head. See 3.
2b—Fls all ray or all disc fls in any one head. See 7.

3a—Papery bract around *each* ray and disc fl in some species or *only* around the ray fls. *Heliantheae.*
3b—No bract surrounding each flower in head. See 4.

4a—Plants strongly scented, lvs finely dissected. *Anthemideae.*
4b—Plants not strongly scented or lvs as above. See 5.

5a—Stigma tips pointed and hairs on the tips. *Astereae.*
5b—Stigma tips cut off (blunt). See 6.

6a—Few broad bristles or none on top of achene (seed). *Helenieae.*

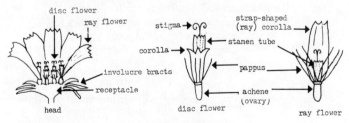

Fig. 163

[167]

6b—Many fine long feathery bristles attached to top of achene. *Senecioneae.*

7a—All fls in head are ray fls, milky sap. *Cichorieae.*
7b—All fls in head of disc type. *Inuleae* and exceptions.

Key to the Tribe Cynareae (Thistles)

1a—Lf edges not spiny, fl heads spiny, yellow. *Centaurea solstitalis.*
1b—Lf edges and fl heads both spiny. See 2.

2a—Lvs shiny green with white veins. *Silybum.*
2b—Lvs dull green, not white veined. See 3.

3a—Low cluster of lvs next to ground. *Cirsium drummondii.*
3b—Plants with upright stems. See 4.

4a—Upper lf surface and stems white haired. *C. californicum.*
4b—Upper lvs slightly haired or none. See 5.

5a—Base of lf extending down stem. *C. vulgare.*
5b—Base of lf not extending down stem. *C. andersonii.*

Genus *Centaurea*

Centaurea solstitalis—Yellow Star Thistle. Pl. 13*e.* Stem much-branched, 3–7 dm tall; lvs narrow extending down stems as wings, whitish surface; fl heads with long yellowish spines, fls yellow. Common, many disturbed places. FW, C, MCF. Most of year.

Introduced from Europe.

> 1 millimeter
> 10 millimeters = 1 centimeter = 13/32 inch
> 10 centimeters = 1 decimeter = ca. 4 inches
> 10 decimeters = 1 meter = 3.3 feet

Fig. 164 Metric scale 1:1

Fig. 165 *Cirsium californicum*   Fig. 166 *Madia elegans*

Genus *Silybum*

Silybum marianum—Milk Thistle. Plant very tall, 1–2 m; lvs shiny green with white veins; fl heads purple, frequent in disturbed places. FW, C, MCF. June–Oct.

Introduced from Europe. Only thistle with milky juice.

Genus *Cirsium*

Cirsium drummondii—Dwarf Thistle. (See p. 22.) Fl heads white to lavender amid low circle of spiny lvs. Frequent in meadows below 12000. MM. June–Aug.

Indians ate the roots raw or roasted. It is the food plant for the Painted Lady or Thistle Butterfly.

C. californicum—Bigelow Thistle. Fig. 165. Stems slender, 5–18 dm tall; upper leaves densely white-wooly; fl heads large red to whitish. Frequent below 7000. FW, C, MCF. April–July.

Named for John Bigelow who was the surgeon and botanist on the Mexican Boundary and Pacific Railway surveys.

[169]

C. vulgare—Bull Thistle. Stem 6–12 dm tall; lvs green above, slightly hairy, lf bases extending as wings down stem; fl heads purple. Common in disturbed places. FW, C, MCF, MM. June–Sept.

Introduced from Europe.

C. andersonii—Anderson's Thistle. Stems slender, purplish-red, 4–9 dm tall; upper lf surface slightly hairy; fls rose-purple in a large head. Dry open areas, 4000–10500. MCF, MM, S. June–Oct.

Key to the Tribe Heliantheae (Sunflowers)

1a—Papery bract only around the seeds of the outer ray fls of a fl head. *Madia elegans*.
1b—Papery bract around seeds of all ray and disc fls in a fl head. See 2.

2a—All disc fls of a head in a flat plane. See 3.
2b—All disc fls on a pronounced cone. See 8.

3a—Distinct petiole as long as lf blade. *Balsamorhiza deltoidea*.
3b—Lf petiole short or absent. See 4.

4a—Seeds fat, rounded. *Helianthella californica*.
4b—Seeds long and narrow. See 5.

5a—Lvs long and narrow. *Wyethia angustifolia*.
5b—Lvs broad. See 6.

6a—Lvs dark shiny green. *W. bolanderi*.
6b—Lvs with white felt surface. See 7.

7a—Lvs oblong, whitish. *W. mollis*.
7b—Lvs delta shaped. *W. invenusta*.

8a—Cone (disc) fls greenish yellow. *Rudbeckia californica*.
8b—Cone fls purple-brown. *R. hirta*.

Indians used the seeds of many species in this tribe for making flour, usually parching them first to remove hairs and chaff.

Genus *Madia*

Madia elegans—Common Madia. Fig. 166. Plants of various heights, 2–8 dm tall, branching near top; ray fls yellow or with maroon blotch at base, fl head opens in evening and closes late next morning. Common in masses about dry opening below 6000 on w. slope. FW, C, MCF, MM. May–Aug.

Genus *Balsamorhiza*

Balsamorhiza deltoidea—Deltoid Balsamroot. Pl. 12*a*. Lvs large, arrowhead-shaped with long petioles, in clumps; fl heads large, yellow. Deep soil of open places below 7000. FW, MCF. April–June.

Indians sometimes ate the leaves raw or the roots baked. They made a chewing gum from the sap.

Genus *Helianthella*

Helianthella californica var. *nevadensis*—California Helianthella. Pl. 12*b*. Plants 2–6 dm tall; lvs mostly attached basally, linear to 25 cm long; fl heads single, yellow; seeds fat, rounded. Dry open areas below 7000 on w. slope. FW, C, MCF, MM. May–Sept.

Genus *Wyethia*

Wyethia angustifolia—Narrow-leaved Mule's Ear. Fig. 167. Stem 2–6 dm tall; upper lvs reduced, lvs linear 2–6 dm long; fl heads yellow, 1–2 per stem; seeds narrowly elongated. Open grassy places below 5500 on w. slope. FW, C, MCF. April–July.

The genus is named for Nathaniel Wyeth, a fur trader who was the first American in what is now southern Idaho.

W. mollis—Mountain Mule's Ear. Pl. 11*f*. Stem 4–10 dm tall; lvs oblong 2–4 dm long, whitish becoming smooth in age; fl heads yellow, 1–4 per stem. Dry open slopes below 10000 on both sides of the Sierra. MCF, MM, S, PJ, SS. May–Aug.

This plant spreads rapidly if the fragile soil surfaces of the Sierra are disturbed. The large masses of Mule's Ear seen along

[171]

Fig. 167 *Wyethia angustifolia*

the east slope are the result of excessive grazing of sheep during the late 1800s and early 1900s. Children often play "mule" by holding a leaf on each side of their heads.

W. bolanderi—Bolander's Wyethia. Pl. 11g. (See p. 110.) Plant low to ground, 1–3 dm tall; lvs dark shiny green, ovate, 4–12 cm long; fl heads large, yellow. Open

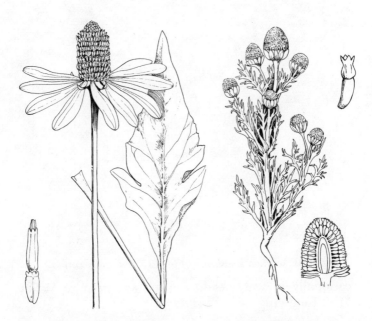

Fig. 168 *Rudbeckia californica*   Fig. 169 *Matricaria matricarioides*

dry places below 4000 on w. slope. FW, C. March–May.

W. invenusta—Coville's Wyethia. (See p. 93.) Stem 3–8 dm tall; lvs delta-shaped, 15–20 cm long; fl heads solitary, yellow; seeds narrowly elongate. Open woods, 3500–6000, on w. slope, Fresno Co. and south. FW, MCF. July–Aug.

Genus *Rudbeckia*

Rudbeckia californica—California Cone Flower. Fig. 168. Stems 6–18 dm tall, unbranched, fls yellow, ray, on a large domelike cone with greenish yellow disc fls. Wet semi-shaded springy places, 5000–8000 on w. slope. MM, MCF. July–Aug.

R. hirta var. *pulcherrima*—Black-eyed Susan. Stem 3–8 dm tall, unbranched; fls prominent, yellow, ray. Oc-

Fig. 170 *Achillea lanulosa*   Fig. 171 *Anthemis cotula*

casionally in wet meadows such as Yosemite Valley, MM. June–Aug.

Introduced from eastern United States.

Key to the Tribe Anthemideae (Mayweed)

1a—Plants small, cone of tiny yellowish fls, disc only. *Matricaria matricarioides.*
1b—Plants 1 dm or taller. See 2.

2a—Ray fls short, 2–4 mm long. *Achillea lanulosa.*
2b—Ray fls longer, 5–12 mm. *Anthemis cotula.*

Genus *Matricaria*

Matricaria matricarioides—Pineapple Weed. Fig. 169. Stems branched, usually less than 1 dm tall; lvs pinnatified, ill smelling; fls tiny, yellow-green, in cones like miniature pineapples. Very common. FW, MCF. Most of year.

Genus *Achillea*

Achillea lanulosa—White Yarrow. Fig. 170. Stems 5–10

dm tall, usually not branched; lvs many, pinnate; fls many, white, in a flat topped group, ray petals 2–4 mm long, strong smelling. Most communities. FW, C, MCF. May–Sept.

Indians used leaves for a general tonic or crushed them and applied them to sores.

Genus *Anthemis*

Anthemis cotula—Mayweed or Dog Fennel. Fig. 171. Stem 1–5 dm tall; lvs pinnate, ill-smelling; fls with white ray petals 5–12 mm long. Common in large masses in disturbed places. FW, C, MCF. April–Aug.

Key to the Tribe *Astereae* (Asters)

1a—Fls yellow, lvs narrow. See 2.
1b—Fls blue, white, or pink. See 5.

2a—Alpine cushion plant. See 3.
2b—Plants from below alpine zone. See 4.

3a—Lf edges saw-toothed. *Haplopappus apargioides.*
3b—Lf edges smooth. *H. acaulis.*

4a—Lf edges saw-toothed. *Grindelia camporum.*
4b—Lf edges smooth. *Solidago occidentalis.*

5a—Bracts surrounding fl head in 3 or more distinct rows. See 6.
5b—Bracts surrounding fl head in 1 row or sometimes 2. See 10.

6a—Plants low tufted, alpine. *Aster peirsonii.*
6b—Plants erect, subalpine or lower. See 7.

7a—Fls light pink. *A. alpigenus* subsp. *andersonii.*
7b—Fls purple-violet. See 8.

8a—Lower lvs narrow, linear. *A. adscendens.*
8b—Lower lvs oblanceolate. See 9.

9a—Lower lvs. clasping main stem. *A. integrifolius.*
9b—Lower lvs not as above. *A. occidentalis.*

10a—Lf tip divided 3 to many times. See 11.
10b—Lf tip not divided. See 12.

Fig. 172 *Grindelia camporum*   Fig. 173 *Solidago occidentalis*

11a—Lf tip divided 3 times. *Erigeron vagus.*
11b—Lf tip divided 5 to many times. *E. compositus.*

12a—Stems erect. See 13.
12b—Low cushion plants of alpine zone. See 15.

13a—Ray fls short 2–3 mm long. *E. lonchophyllus.*
13b—Ray fls longer, 5–25 mm long. See 14.

14a—Lvs longest at base of stem. *E. peregrinus.*
14b—Lvs same size up stem. *E. breweri.*

15a—Lvs with 3 prominent veins. *E. nevadincola.*
15b—Lvs with 1 main vein. See 16.

16a—Stems tall, 5–20 cm tall, fls blue. *E. clokeyi.*
16b—Stem short, 1–5 cm, fls deep purple. *E. pygmaeus.*

Genus *Haplopappus*

Haplopappus apargioides—Alpine Pynocoma. Plant low cushionlike; lvs narrow with toothed edges; fls yellow. 7500–12000, common. A. July–Sept.

Fig. 174 *Aster integrifolius*

H. acaulis—Cushion Stenotus. Pl. 11*e*. Plant low, cushionlike; lvs linear with smooth edges; fls yellow. Dry open places 5000–11000 on e. slope. S, A. May–Aug.

Genus *Grindelia*

Grindelia camporum—Great Valley Gumplant. Fig. 172. Stems clumped, 5–12 dm tall; lvs narrow with edges saw-toothed; fls yellow, the fl head white, gummy. Frequent in open places on w. slope. FW, C. May–Oct.

Genus *Solidago*

Solidago occidentalis—Western Goldenrod. Fig. 173. Stems much branched from creeping rootstock, 6–20 dm tall; lvs narrow, edges smooth; fl heads many, small, yellow. Common most communities. July–Nov.

[177]

Fig. 175 *Erigeron compositus*

Genus *Aster*

Aster peirsonii—Peirson's Aster. Stem low, hairless with tufted linear lvs; fls purple or violet. Meadows, 11000–13000, Tioga Pass and south. A. July–Sept.

A. alpigenus subsp. *andersonii*—Anderson's Alpine Aster. Pl. 12c. Stem tall, 1–4 dm with tufted basal lvs, oblanceolate; fls ray, light pink. Wet or boggy meadows, 4000–11500, Common. MM, S. June–Sept.

A. adscencens—Long-leaved Aster. Stems slender, erect, 2–7 dm tall; lvs linear; fls violet or purple. Dryish meadows below 7500, mostly on e. slope. MM. July–Oct.

[178]

A. integrifolius—Entire-leaved Aster. Fig. 174. Stems several, stout, 2–7 dm tall; lvs oblanceolate with basal wings clasping stem; fl head large, purple-violet. Dry meadows and open woods, 5500–11000. MM, MCF, S. July–Sept.

A. occidentalis—Western Mountain Aster. Stem erect, 2–5 dm tall, often reddish; lower lf base not clasping stem; fls lavender or violet. Moist open places, 4000–11000, widespread. MM, MCF. July–Sept.

Genus *Erigeron*

Erigeron vagus—Loose Daisy. Plant low, branching, cushionlike; lvs with 3-lobed tips, wooly haired; fls rose colored or whitish. 1000–14000, loose rock, common. S, A. July–Aug.

E. compositus—Cut-leaved Daisy. Fig. 175. Plant low, cushionlike; lf tips much divided like a fan; fls white, pink, or bluish. Rocky slopes 8000–13000, common. S, A. July–Aug.

Spreads rapidly when an area is overgrazed.

E. lonchophyllus—Short-rayed Daisy. Stems slender, 1–6 dm tall; lvs linear; fls ray, short, 2–3 mm long, white or pale lavender. Moist meadows, 6000–12000, widespread. MM. July–Aug.

E. peregrinus—Wandering Daisy. Stem to 7 dm tall; lvs mostly oblanceolate about base; fls ray, rose-purple to occasionally white. Meadows 5500–11000, widespread. MM. July–Sept.

E. breweri—Brewer's Daisy. (See p. 58.) Stems slender, erect to trailing 1–3 dm; lvs numerous, linear, to top of stem; fls ray, blue, 4–10 mm long. Dry rocky places, 5000–11000, widespread. MM, S, A. July–Aug.

E. nevadincola—Nevada Daisy. Plant low, coarse, cushionlike; lvs linear, each with 3 prominent parallel

[179]

veins; fls white to blue-lavender. Rocky slopes on e. side of Sierra, 6000–7500. PJ, MCF. June–July.

E. clokeyi–Clokey's Daisy. Plant low, cushionlike; lvs linear; fl stem leafy; fls lavender. 8000–11000, southern Sierra. MCF, S. June–Aug.

E. pygmaeus–Dwarf Daisy. Pl. 13*b*. Plant low, compact, cushionlike; lvs linear; fl stem leafless; fls purple or lavender. Rocky places, 10000–13000. A. July–Aug.

Key to the Tribe Helenieae (Sneezeweed)

1a–Lvs deeply dissected. *Eriophyllum lanatum*.
1b–Lvs various but not toothed. See 2.

2a–Lvs alternate. See 3.
2b–Lvs opposite. See 6.

3a–Moist meadows. See 4.
3b–Dry alpine slopes. See 5.

4a–3–8 fls per stalk. *Helenium hoopesii*.
4b–1 fl per stalk. *H. bigelovii*.

5a–Lvs spoon-shaped, densely white. *Hulsea vesita*.
5b–Lvs linear, slightly toothed, green. *H. algida*.

6a–Tall plants 15–35 cm. *Whitneya dealbata*.
6b–Low plants, 2–10 cm. *Lasthenia chrysostoma*.

Genus *Eriophyllum*

Eriophyllum lanatum–Common Wooly Sunflower. Pl. 17*d*. Stem branched, 1–8 dm tall from woody base; lvs pinnatified and mostly near base, white wooly covering; fls many, yellow, 6–15 mm wide. Very common late spring and summer, 9000 or lower. FW, C, MCF, MM, S. May–Aug.

Genus *Helenium*

Helenium hoopesii–Tall Mountain Helenium Pl. 12*e*. Stems several, 4–10 dm tall; lvs oblanceolate to 3 dm; fls yellow to orangish. Meadows and other open moist places, 7500–11000. MM. July–Sept.

Indians crushed the flowers to make an inhalent for hay fever. The Dainty Yellow Butterfly uses species of this genus as food plants.

H. bigelovii—Bigelow's Sneezeweed. Pl. 12*g*. (See p. 169.) Stems single or clumps, 4–8 cm tall; lvs alternate, oblanceolate to 22 cm long and 4 cm wide; fl head a round ball of dark disc fls and a fringe of yellow ray fls, usually 1 per stalk. Moist meadows, 3000–10000, widespread. MM. June–Aug.

Genus *Hulsea*

Hulsea vestita—Pumice Hulsea. Lvs tufted, spoonshaped, 2–5 cm long, densely white; fl heads large, yellow, tinted red. Sandy volcanic or granitic soils in open areas, 6000–11000. MCF, MM. June–Aug.

H. algida—Alpine Hulsea. Pl. 13*a*. Lvs tufted, linear, to 15 cm long, edges slightly toothed; fl heads large, yellow. Rocky slopes, 10000–14000. A. July–Aug.

Genus *Whitneya*

Whitneya dealbata—Whitneya. (See p. 151.) Stems single or few, 15–35 cm tall; lvs opposite and whitish; fls yellow, single or few per plant. Open areas of forest 4000–7000, Yosemite and north. MCF. June–Aug.

Genus *Lasthenia*

Lasthenia chrysostoma—Goldfields. Annual. Plant low; lvs linear in opposite arrangements, 2–10 cm tall; fls gold, growing in very large masses or sheets, giving open and semi-open areas a gold carpeting. Common on w. slope below 4000. FW. March–May.

Key to the Tribe Senecioneae (Groundsel)

1a—Lvs alternately arranged. See 2.
1b—Lvs oppositely arranged. See 7.

2a—Most of lvs basal and rapidly reduced up stem. See 3.
2b—Lvs slightly reduced if at all up stem. See 5.

3a—Stem a single stalk. 3–20 dm tall. *Senecio integerrimus.*
3b—Few to several stems, often shorter. See 4.

4a—Lvs densely white-wooly. *S. canus.*
4b—Lvs slightly hairy to none. *S. scorzonella.*

5a—Stems low, less than 3 dm tall. *S. fremontii.*
5b—Stems taller than 3 dm. See 6.

6a—Lvs triangular. *S. triangularis.*
6b—Lvs pinnately lobed. *S. clarkianus.*

7a—5–12 pairs of opposite lvs per stem. See 8.
7b—2–4 pairs of opposite lvs per stem. See 10.

8a—Lf edges toothed, somewhat delta-shaped. *Arnica amplexicaulis.*
8b—Lf edges smooth, lanceolate-shaped. See 9.

9a—1-stemmed plants. *A. chamissonis.*
9b—Several tufted stems. *A. longifolia.*

10a—Lvs heart-shaped. *A. cordifolia.*
10b—Lower lvs oblong to ovate. See 11.

11a—Bristles at top of seed white. *A. nevadensis.*
11b—Bristles at top of seed brownish. *A. mollis.*

Genus *Senecio*

The genus *Senecio* is one of the largest in the world with over 2000 species.

Senecio integerrimus var. *major*—Single-stemmed Butterweed. Pl. 12f. Stems stout, single, 3–9 dm tall, leafy only near base; lvs spoon-shaped; fl heads yellow in flat topped cluster. Wooded slopes below 11000, very common. FW, C, MCF. May–Aug.

S. canus—Wooly Butterweed. Stem low, 1–3 dm, forming mats of grayish to white lvs; lvs reduced on upper stem; fl heads yellow. Dry places, 4000–12000, southern Sierra. MCF, S. May–Aug.

S. scorzonella—Sierra Butterweed. Stems 2–5 dm tall; lvs tufted, oblanceolate, edges toothed; 10–30 yellow fl heads in compact group. Moist open places, 6000–11000, widespread. MM. July–Aug.

[182]

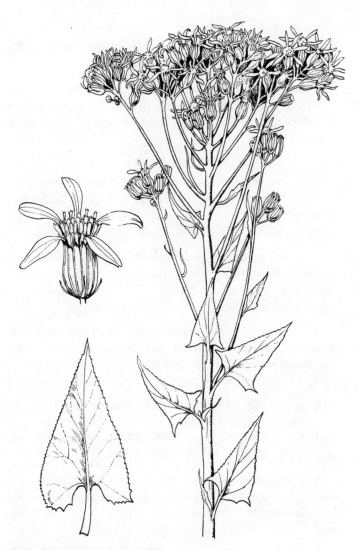

Fig. 176 *Senecio triangularis*

S. fremontii – Dwarf Mountain Butterweed. Stem branched, 1–1.5 dm tall; lvs spatula-shaped, teeth at tip. Near rocks, 8500–13000. A. July–Sept.

S. triangularis–Arrowhead Butterweed. Fig. 176. Stems tall, 5–15 dm; lvs arrowhead-shaped up entire stem, edges toothed. Wet shady places, 4000–12000, mostly on e. slope. MCF, S. July–Sept.

S. *clarkianus*—Clark's Butterweed. Stem 6–12 dm tall; lvs deeply lobed, leafy to top of stem; fl heads yellow. Moist places, 7000–9000, Yosemite south. MCF. July–Aug.

Genus *Arnica*

Arnica amplexicaulis—Streambank Arnica. Stems 3–7 dm tall; lvs in 5–12 opposite pairs, elliptic to lanceolate-shaped with toothed margins; fl heads yellow. Moist stream banks, 7000–10000. MCF, MM. July–Aug.

A. *chamissonis* subsp. *foliosa*—Meadow Arnica. Stems single, 3–8 dm tall; lvs opposite in 5–10 pairs, lanceolate-shaped; fl head yellow. Moist meadows, 5000–11000, Tioga Pass region and north. MM. July–Aug.

A. *longifolia* subsp. *myriadenia*—Seep-spring Arnica. Stems tufted, 3–6 dm tall; lvs opposite in 5–7 pairs, lanceolate-shaped; fl heads yellow. Wet springy places, 5000–11000, scattered locations. MM, MCF. July–Aug.

A. *cordifolia*—Heart-leaved Arnica. Stem usually single, 2–6 dm tall; lvs basal, heart-shaped with edges toothed; fl heads yellow. 3500–10000, mostly Yosemite and north. MCF, MM, S. May–Aug.

A. *nevadensis*—Sierra Arnica. Stem 1–2.5 dm tall; lvs ovate, 3–8 cm long, opposite in 2–3 pairs; fl heads yellow, bristles at top of seed white. Rocky stream banks, 6000–12000. MCF. July–Aug.

A. *mollis*—Cordilleran Arnica. Pl. 13c. Stem 2–6 dm tall; lvs basal, lanceolate, stem lvs opposite in 3–4 pairs; fl head yellow, bristles at top of seed brownish. Widespread, 7500–11500. MM. July–Sept.

Key to the Tribe Cichorieae (Chicory)

1a—Fls yellow-orange. See 2.
1b—Fls purple, blue, or pink. See 10.

2a—Hairs at top of seeds whitish or absent. See 3.
2b—Hairs at top of seeds many, yellowish. See 9.

3a—Plants tall, 5–25 dm. *Sonchus oleraceus.*
3b—Plants lower, 1–4 dm tall. See 4.

4a—Lvs lying flat, broad. *Taraxacum officinale.*
4b—Lvs nearly upright, linear. See 5.

5a—Petals at right angle to fl head. See 6.
5b—Petals parallel (upright) to fl head. See 7.

6a—Lvs narrow, small reversed teeth. *Microseris.*
6b—Lvs broad, teeth pointed towards tip. *Nothocalais alpestris.*

7a—Fls yellow. See 8.
7b—Fls orangish. *Agoseris aurantiaca.*

8a—Lvs long linear. *A. glauca.*
8b—Lvs semipinnate, reverse pointed. *A. retrorsa.*

9a—Fls white. *Hieracium albiflorum.*
9b—Fls yellow. *H. horridum.*

10a—Fls purple. *Tragopogon porrifolius.*
10b—Fls not purple. See 11.

11a—Fls light blue. *Cichorium intybus.*
11b—Fls pink. *Stephanomeria lactucina.*

Genus *Sonchus*

Sonchus oleraceus—Common Sow Thistle. Stem single, 5–25 dm tall; lvs lyrate (toothed like a comb), with lower lobes clasped about stem; fl heads many, yellow, with milky sap, each fl head becoming a white fluffy seed head. Frequent in disturbed places, FW, C, MCF. Most of year.

Introduced from Europe. Not a true thistle. The young leaves may be eaten as a salad green or cooked like spinach, but they have a somewhat bitter taste. It is often eaten in Europe, and Indians adopted it after it spread in America.

Genus *Taraxacum*

Taraxacum officinale—Dandelion. Lvs in basal cluster,

[185]

Fig. 177 *Hieracium albiflorum*   Fig. 178 *Raillardella scaposa*

oblong-shaped with toothed edges; fls bright yellow-orange. Widespread, all communities. Most of year.

Introduced from Europe. The common name is from the French *dent de lion* = Lion's tooth. It can be eaten like the Common Sow Thistle and is an important food source for many birds, rabbits, and chipmunks.

Genus *Microseris*

Microseris nutans—Nodding Scorzonella. Stem 1–4.5 dm tall; lvs nearly all basal, linear with entire to deeply toothed edges; fls with yellow petals at right angles to fl head, milky sap. Moist semi-shaded places, 4000–9500. MCF. June–Aug.

Genus *Nothocalais*

Nothocalais alpestris—Alpine Lake Dandelion. Lvs basal, slightly toothed, milky sap; fl head solitary, yellow,

[186]

Genus *Agoseris*

1–2 dm scape. Damp meadows, 7000–12000. MCF, MM. July–Aug.

Agoseris aurantiaca—Orange-flowered Agoseris. Stem 1–5 dm tall; lvs at base, linear with occasional teeth; fls burnt-orange on leafless stem. Semi-dry open places, 6000–11000. MCF. July–Aug.

A. *glauca* var. *monticola*—Short-beaked Agoseris. Stem 1–3 dm tall; lvs basal, linear; fls yellow, milky sap. Dry open areas and edges of meadows, 5000–11000, widespread. MCF, MM. July–Aug.

A. *retrorsa*—Reverse-pointed Agoseris. Pl. 13*d*. Lvs basal, margin lobes pointed toward base of lf; fl scape 1.5–5 dm tall; fls yellow, milky sap. Dry open places below 8000. MCF, MM. May–Aug.

Genus *Hieracium*

Hieracium albiflorum—White-flowered Hawkweed. Fig. 177. Stem 4–8 dm tall; lvs mostly basal, 8–15 cm long, usually covered with yellowish hairs. fls white. Dry open woods below 11000. MCF. June–Aug.

Indians used the sap as a chewing gum. A centuries-old belief is that hawks eat the milky sap to sharpen their eyesight.

H. horridum—Shaggy Hawkweed. Stem 1–3.5 dm tall, with dense shaggy yellowish hairs; lvs oblong, 3–10 cm long; fl heads many, bright yellow, milky sap. Dry open areas, 5000–11000. MCF, MM. July–Aug.

Genus *Tragopogon*

Tragopogon porrifolius—Salsify or Oyster Plant. Pl. 13*g*. Stems usually in clumps, 6–12 dm tall; lvs narrowly linear; fls purple, milky sap. A frequent plant in open disturbed places. FW, MCF. April–June.

Introduced from Europe. Indians and others have used the milky sap for chewing gum, as a remedy for indigestion, and have also applied it to sores. The young leaves can be used in salads, and the roots when cooked taste like oysters.

Genus *Cichorium*

Cichorium intybus—Chicory. Stems several, 3–10 dm tall; lvs large, oblong, basal, becoming much reduced upward on stem; fls many, light blue, close to stem. Frequent in disturbed places. FW, MCF. June–Oct.

Introduced from Europe. The dried root is used as a coffee additive or substitute in Europe and the southern United States. The young leaves can also be used as salad greens.

Genus *Stephanomeria*

Stephanomeria lactucina—Large-flowered Stephanomeria. Stems single, 1–3 dm tall; lvs linear 1–3 cm long, occasionally toothed, upper lvs reduced; fls pink, milky sap. Dry flats, 4000–8000, Yosemite north. MM. July–Aug.

Key to the Tribe Inuleae and exceptions

1a—Fl head of small rounded white to rosy papery bracts. *Antennaria rosea*.
1b—Fl head of elongated bracts, not papery. See 2.

2a—Bracts surrounding each fl head black tipped. See 7.
2b—Bracts surrounding each fl head not black tipped. See 3.

3a—Lvs linear or ovate. See 3.
3b—Lvs pinnately tooth. See 5.

4a—Lvs linear. See 4.
4b—Lvs ovate. *Chrysopis breweri*.

5a—Lvs green. *Raillardella scaposa*.
5b—Lvs silky. *R. argentea*.

6a—Lvs 2–7 cm long. *Chaenactis alpigena*.
6b—Lvs 15–60 cm long. *C. douglasii*.

7a—Coarsely toothed lvs to top of stem. *Senecio vulgaris*.
7b—Large basal lvs only. *S. aronicoides*.

Genus *Antennaria*

Antennaria rosea—Rosy Everlasting or Pussytoes. Pl.

13f. Stems usually many, grayish, forming a large leafy mat, 0.5–2.5 dm tall, with scattered alternate lvs; fl heads rounded papery bracts with a pinkish to rose color. Common in open areas below 12000. MM. April–Aug.

The sap can be chewed like gum. Seeds are eaten by birds, rabbits, mice, and deer. The caterpillars of the Virginia Lady Butterfly use the plant as food.

Genus *Chrysopis*

Chrysopis breweri—Brewer's Golden Aster. (See p. 58.) Stems few to 20, erect, 2–8 dm tall; lvs ovate, alternately arranged on stem; fl heads golden. Open slopes and semi-open woods, 4500–11000, common. MCF. July–Sept.

Genus *Raillardella*

Raillardella scaposa—Green Leaved Raillardella. Fig. 178. Plant low tuft of thin linear lvs 3–15 cm long; fl heads green, yellow, disc, on leafless stalk. Dry open places, 6500–11000. MCF, S, A. July–Aug.

R. argentea—Silky Raillardella. Plant low tuft of linear lvs, conspicuously gray-silky; disc fl heads yellow. Open rocky places, 9000–12000. S, A. July–Aug.

Genus *Chaenactis*

Chaenactis alpigena—Southern Sierra Chaenactis. Plant dense mat; lvs densely yellow haired, with a few pinnate lobes, fl head of creamy-white disc fls. Open sandy flats, 8500–12000, widespread. S, A. July–Aug.

C. douglasii—Hoary Chaenactis. Fig. 179. Lvs all basal; stem loosely branched, 1.5–6 dm tall; each lf with 4–8 pairs of leaflets, somewhat wooly; disc fl heads, whitish to pink. Open sandy or rocky slopes, 3000–11000. FW, MCF, PJ, SS. June–July.

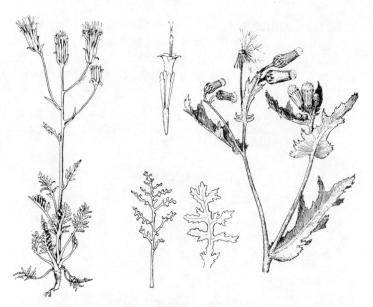

Fig. 179 *Chaenactis douglasii*   Fig. 180 *Senecio vulgaris*

Genus *Senecio*

Senecio vulgaris—Common Butterweed or Old Man In Spring. Fig. 180. Stem usually single, 1–5 dm tall; lvs coarsely toothed, along entire stem; fl heads small yellow. Extremely common all year in disturbed places. FW, C, MCF. All year.

S. aronicoides—California Butterweed. Similar to *S. intergerrimus* except the yellow fl heads are without ray

    1 millimeter
    10 millimeters = 1 centimeter = 13/32 inch
    10 centimeters = 1 decimeter = ca. 4 inches
    10 decimeters = 1 meter = 3.3 feet

Fig. 181 Metric scale 1:1

Fig. 182 *Sparganium simplex*

fls. (See p. 182.) Frequent in open places such as woods.
logged areas, and burns. Below 8000. MCF. April–July.

KEY TO THE CLASS MONOCOTYLEDONEAE

1a—Long grasslike lvs floating in ponds, white fls in
    round balls. *Sparganiaceae.* See p. 192.
1b—Plant not grasslike. See 2.

2a—Large arrowhead-shaped lvs. *Alismataceae.* p. 192.
2b—Lvs various not as in 2a. See 3.

3a—Ovary superior. See 4.
3b—Ovary inferior. See 5.

4a—Fls in racemes or panicles. *Liliaceae,* p. 192.
4b—Fls in an umbel on leafless stalk. *Amaryllidaceae,*
    p. 198.

5a—Fls regular, lvs flat, irislike. *Iridaceae,* p. 202.
5b—Fls irregular. *Orchidaceae,* p. 203.

[191]

FAMILY ALISMATACEAE
(WATER PLANTAIN)

Genus *Sagittaria*

Sagittaria cuneata—Arrow Head Plant. Lvs strongly arrowhead-shaped; fls with 3 white petals. Shallow water below 7500. June–Sept.

Indians boiled or roasted the tuberous roots and ate them with meat or fish. The tubers are also a principal food of ducks and geese.

FAMILY SPARGANIACEAE (BUR REED)

Sparganium simplex—Pond Bur Reed. Fig. 182. Stems long, slender; stems and lvs float gracefully on mountain ponds; easily recognized by the floating lvs and 3–6 round burlike heads. Ponds and shallow lakes, 4000–12000. ML. June–Sept.

Indians and the early Greeks cooked the tubers for food. Also the Greeks claimed that seeds and roots soaked in wine were good for snake bite. This is an important waterfowl food.

KEY TO THE FAMILY LILIACEAE (LILY)

1a—Sepals and petals unlike in color, size, and shape. See 2.

1b—Both sepals and petals similar in color and shape. See 8.

2a—Fls rounded, hanging downward. *Calochortus albus.*

2b—Fls cup shaped and upright. See 3.

3a—Plants low to ground, less than 2 dm. See 4.

3b—Plants on tall stems 2–6 dm. See 6.

4a—Fls bright yellow. *C. monophyllus.*

4b—Fls whitish. See 5.

5a—Petal tips sharp pointed. *C. minimus.*

5b—Petal tips flat or rounded. *C. nudus.*

6a—Dark spot on petal surrounded by yellow. *C. super-bus.*

6b—Petal with middle green strip on outside. See 7.

7a—Yellow gland area round. *C. nuttallii.*
7b—Yellow gland area triangular. *C. leichtlinii.*

8a—Lvs all or mostly basal. See 9.
8b—Lvs along entire stem. See 14.

9a—Fls light to dark blue. *Camassia leichtlinii.*
9b—Fls whitish. See 10.

10a—2–5 ovate lvs. See 11.
10b—Many narrow lvs. See 12.

11a—Lvs green, no spots. *Clintonia uniflora.*
11b—Lvs green with brownish spots. *Erythronium.*

12a—Main fl stem leafy. *Zigadenus venenosus.*
12b—Main fl stem nearly leafless. See 13.

13a—Open areas of low w. foothills. *Chlorogalum.*
13b—Dry shaded fir woods. *Xerophyllum tenax.*

14a—Lvs alternate or opposite. See 15.
14b—Lvs in whorls along stem. *Lilium.*

15a—Low slender-stemmed, 1–8 dm tall. See 16.
15b—Tall coarse-leaved plants, 1–2 m. *Veratrum.*

16a—Lvs narrow linear. *Fritillaria atropurpurea.*
16b—Lvs ovate-oblong. See 17.

17a—Fls nearly tubular. *Disporum hookeri.*
17b—Fls open starlike. *Smilacina stellata.*

Genus *Calochortus* (Mariposa Tulip)

Indians ate the bulbs of this genus raw or roasted. Attempts to grow the mariposa tulip in gardens have met with little success. The Spanish word *mariposa* = butterfly.

Calochortus albus—Fairy Lantern or Globe Lily. Pl. 14*a*.

Fig. 183 *Calochortus monophyllus*   Fig. 184 *Disporum hookeri*

Stems 2–8 dm tall; fls a white globe hanging downward, sometimes pinkish. Frequent in shady woods below 5000 on w. slope. FW, C, MCF. April–June.

C. amoenus—Rosy Fairy Lantern. Similar to *C. albus* but with dark rose fls. Occurs along the edge of foothills from Madera Co. south.

C. monophyllus—Yellow Star Tulip. Fig. 183. Plant low, 8–20 cm tall; fls deep yellow. Shady woods below 4000 on w. slope. FW, C, PP. April–May.

C. minimus—Lesser Star Tulip. Plant barely above ground; fls white with pointed tips. Openings in woods, 4000–9500. PP, MCF. April–Aug.

C. nudus—Naked Star Tulip. Stem erect 10–25 cm; fls white to pale lavender, petal tip flat to rounded. Damp meadows below 7500 on w. slope. MM, MCF. May–July.

[194]

C. superbus—Superb Tulip. Stem erect, 4–6 dm tall; fls white to yellowish or lavender, dark purplish spot surrounded by yellow on each petal. Dry meadows below 6000 on w. slope. MM. May–July.

C. nuttallii var. *bruneaunis*—Sego Lily. Stem erect, 2–4 dm tall; fls white or tinted lilac, each petal with round yellow spot near the inside base and green strip on outside. Open grassy places below 10000 on e. slope. PJ, MCF. May–Aug.

State flower of Utah.

C. leichtlinii—Leichtlin's Tulip. Pl. 14*b*. Stem erect, 2–4 dm tall; fls white, tinted light blue, a yellow triangular spot at base of each petal. Open places, 4000–11000, widespread. MCF, MM, S. June–Aug.

Named for Max Leichtlin who is known for introducing many wild plants into the gardens of Europe as ornamentals from about 1850 to 1910.

Genus *Camassia*

Camassia leichtlinii—Leichtlin's Camas. Pl. 14*g*. Lvs linear; fls light blue to blue-violet. Wet grassy meadows below 10000, widespread. MM. June–Aug.

Indians considered the bulbs an important food. They first roasted them and then pressed them flat while cooling to speed drying. Whether fresh roasted or eaten later, the bulbs have a delightful vanilla flavor. Indians valued the best growing places so much that many major Indian wars were fought over them. This species can be mistaken for the poisonous Death Camas.

Genus *Clintonia*

Clintonia uniflora—Bride's Bonnet, Queen Cup. Plant is low cluster of 2–3 ovate lvs; fls erect, single, white. Usually in masses under shady shrubs, 3500–6000, on w. slope. MCF. May–June.

Genus *Erythronium*

Erythronium multiscapoideum—Sierra Fawn Lily. Lvs

[195]

few, basal, oblanceolate, 4–10 cm long, spotted brownish like a young fawn; scape 1–2 dm tall; fls large, white to cream. Common under manzanita shrubs below 4000 on w. slope. FW, C. March–April.

Genus *Zigadenus*

Zigadenus venenosus—Death Camus. Pl. 14c. Lvs linear up stem; fls whitish, starlike. Semi-shade to open meadows below 8500. FW, MCF, C. May–July.

Poisonous to cattle and sheep.

Genus *Chlorogalum*

Chlorogalum pomeridianum—Soap Plant. Lvs all basal, with wavy margins; fl stalk very tall, leafless, with many white fls with greenish midveins. Frequent on lower w. slope. FW, C. May–Aug.

Indians split the bulbs and used them like a bar of soap. They crushed the leaves and bulbs for use as a fish stunner. The flowers open in late afternoon and, if a bouquet is placed in a sunny window, they can be tricked into flowering early by pulling the shade down to simulate sunset; the flowers will pop open before your eyes within 1 or 2 minutes.

Genus *Xerophyllum*

Xerophyllum tenax—Bear Grass. Pl. 14d. Lvs in large clumps, wiry, grasslike, with a long fl stalk above, with a mass of tiny white fls. Semi-shady woods below 7000, Placer Co. and north. MCF. May–Aug.

Indians used the wiry leaves in making baskets.

Genus *Veratrum*

Veratrum californicum—Corn Lily. Pl. 14e. Stems tall, coarse, 1–2 m high, with many large lvs; fls creamwhite. Damp to dry loose-soiled meadows below 11000. MM. June–Aug.

Incorrectly called Skunk Cabbage, which does not occur in the Sierra. True Skunk Cabbage is a low yellow-bracted plant known only from Mendocino Co. and north along the coast. Indian women made a tea from the fresh roots of the Corn Lily for birth control.

Genus *Fritillaria*

Fritillaria atropurpurea—Purple Fritillary. Pl. 14*f*. Stem erect, 6 dm or less; lvs linear with waxy bluish covering; fls greenish to purplish-brown with yellow spots. Semi-shade below 10500. MCF. April–July.

Genus *Disporum*

Disporum hookeri var. *trachyandrum*—Hooker's Fairy Bell. Fig. 184. (See p. 152.) Stem arching, 3–8 dm long, with small white tubular fls at end. Shaded wet springy places, 4000–8000, widespread. MCF. April–July.

Genus *Smilacina*

Smilacina stellata—False Solomon's Seal. Pl. 15*a*. Stem arching, 3–6 dm long, with tiny white fls at end, later becoming red berries. Dry shaded woods below 7000. MCF. April–July.

Indians used dried powdered root to stop bleeding.

Key to the Genus *Lilium* (Lily)

1a—Fls white. *Lilium washingtonianum.*
1b—Fls variously orange-reddish. See 2.

2a—Plants of dry shaded forest. *L. humboldtii.*
2b—Plants of wet shaded places. See 3.

3a—Fls horizontal or ascending. *L. parvum.*
3b—Fls nodding. See 4.

4a—Fls fragrant. *L. kelleyanum.*
4b—Fls not fragrant. *L. pardalinum.*

The genus *Lilium* has many different species found throughout the temperate mountain regions of the world. The largest number of species are found in the Orient.

Tiger Lily is a name often used for all of the yellowish-orange species. The name comes from an old oriental tale that a tiger wounded by an arrow, was healed by a friendly magician. The two became fast friends and the tiger asked him to use his magic to continue the friendship after his death. Eventually the tiger died of old age and the tiger's body became the tiger lily. Later the magician died and when his body was accidentally washed away in a flood, the tiger lily then spread throughout the world in search of his friend.

California Indians roasted the bulbs for food. Lillies should never be dug as they are very slow growing and do not transplant well.

Lilium washingtonianum—Washington Lily. Stems with tall whorls of shiny green lvs, ½ to 2½ m tall; up to 20 white trumpet fls, fragrant. Dry shady woods, 4000–7000 on w. slope. MCF. July–Aug.

L. humboldtii—Humboldt Lily. Pl. 15*b*. Lvs and stems for *L. washingtonianum*; fls orange-yellow, spotted maroon. Dry shaded woods below 7000 on w. slope. PP, MCF. June–July.

Named for Baron Friedrich von Humboldt, who explored the western hemisphere in the early 1800s.

L. parvum—Alpine Lily. Pl. 15*c*. Stem similar to *L. washingtonianum*, to 20 dm tall; fls bell-shaped orange to dark red with spots, horizontal or upright. Marshy places among alder and willow thickets, 6500–9000. MCF. July–Sept.

L. kelleyanum—Kelly's Lily. Much like *L. pardalinum*, but fls nodding, fragrant. Southern Sierra and along e. slope, wet meadows and swamps. MM. July–Aug.

L. pardalinum—Leopard Lily or Panther Lily. Pl. 14*d*. Stems stout, 1–2½ m tall; fls yellow with some red, spotted, nodding and not fragrant. In large masses about wet springy places below 6000. FW, MM, MCF. May–July.

KEY TO THE FAMILY AMARYLLIDACEAE (AMARYLLIS)

1a—Plants with onion odor. See 2.
1b—Plants without onion odor. See 5.

2a—Growing in wet marshes. *Allium validum*.
2b—Growing in dry places. See 3.

3a—Fl stem 2–5 dm tall, fls white. *A. amplectens*.
3b—Fl stem low. See 4.

4a—Fls pale rose on short stem. *A. campanulatum*.
4b—Fls greenish-white, almost stemless. *A. obtusum*.

5a—Each fl with 6 stamens. See 6.
5b—Each fl with 3 stamens. See 9.

6a—Anthers firmly attached. *Dichelostemma pulchella*.
6b—Anthers swinging freely at tip of filament. See 7.

7a—Fls white. *Triteleia hyacinthina*.
7b—Fls blue or yellow. See 8.

8a—Fls blue. *T. laxa*.
8b—Fls yellow. *T. scabra*.

9a—Fls blue-violet. *Brodiaea elegans*.
9b—Fls pink. *Dichelostemma volubilis*.

Genus *Allium* (Onion)

Bulbs of all onion species are edible, varying in the degree of strongness. Any onion including the cultivated varieties are poisonous if eaten in too large a quantity. Indians used red bulb skins as a dye source.

Allium validum—Swamp Onion. Lvs tall to 1 m, flat; fl stalk with many rose to whitish fls in a terminal ball. Frequent in open wet meadows, 4000–11000. MCF, MM, S. June–Aug.

The name "Onion Valley" has been used for many different valleys in the Sierra, because the early explorers found great masses of Swamp Onions in wet mountain meadows.

A. amplectens—Narrow-leaved Onion. Pl. 15*e*. Stem erect, 2–5 dm tall; 2–4 lvs, narrow; fls many, white to pinkish, on top of leafless stalk. Dry open fields below 6000 on w. slope. FW, C. March–July.

[199]

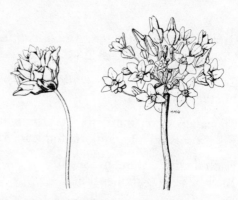

Fig. 185 *Dichelostemma pulchella*   Fig. 186 *Dichelostemma volubilis*

A. campanulatum—Sierra Onion. Stems short, with a round mass of pale rose fls on top of a leafless stalk. Open or semi-shaded dry woods, 2000–9000, common. FW, C, MCF, S. May–July.

A. obtusum—Red Sierra Onion. Plant low to ground, appearing stemless; fls white with purple midveins. Open slopes and flats, 7000–12000. MCF, S. May–Aug.

Species Formerly in Genus Brodiaea

The following six species were previously grouped as the genus *Brodiaea*, named for J. Brodie who was a Scottish botanist. All are known as Indian potato because the solid bulbs were eaten by the Indians raw or roasted and resemble the Irish potato in flavor.

Genus *Dichelostemma*

Dichelostemma pulchella—Blue Dicks or Wild Hyacinth. Fig. 185. Fl stems many, often in large clump. 3–6 dm tall; fls many, dark blue-purple, on a leafless stem, 6 unmovable anthers per flower. Often the first spring wildflower at the lower elevations. FW, C, MCF. Feb–June.

D. volubilis—Snake or Twining Lily. Fig. 186. Stems long, pink, twining up through shrubs; fls many, pink,

[200]

Fig. 187 *Triteleia hyacinthina*   Fig. 188 *Triteleia laxa*

in a ball, 3 firmly anchored stamens per fl. Woodland below 4000 on w. slope. FW, C. March–May.

Genus *Triteleia*

Triteleia hyacinthina—White Triteleia. Fig. 187. Fl stem erect, 3–6 dm tall; fls white or tinted light blue with green midveins in a terminal umbel, 6 movable anthers on ends of filaments. Semi-open fields of w. slope below 6000. FW, C, MCF. April–July.

T. laxa—Wally Basket or Ithuriel's Spear. Pl. 15*f*. Fig. 188. Fl stem very tall, leafless, to 1 m; fls in large terminal umbel, light blue, 6 free-swinging anthers, very common in grassy open places below 5000 on w. slope. FW, C. April–June.

Flower stalks were used by Indians in temporary baskets.

T. scabra—Pretty Face. Pl. 16*a*. Fig. 189. Fl stem leafless, 1–4 dm tall; fls many, short tubular, with petals at right angles to tube, 6 free-swinging anthers. Very common in grassy places below 5000 on w. slope. FW, C. April–June.

T. analina—Similar to *T. scabra*, but more slender stemmed and flowered. Found above 5000. June–Aug.

[201]

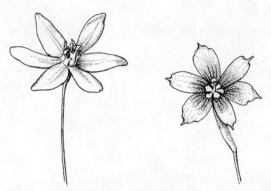

Fig. 189 *Triteleia scabra*   Fig. 190 *Sisyrinchium bellum*

Genus *Brodiaea*

Brodiaea elegans—Harvest Brodiaea. Pl. 16*b*. Fl stem leafless, 1–4 dm tall; fls in terminal umbel, dark blue-violet, 3 firmly attached stamens alternating with 3 white nonfunctional stamens. Open dry grassy places below 7000 on w. slope. FW, C, MCF. April–July.

KEY TO THE FAMILY IRIDACEAE (IRIS)

1a—Fls large, petals 4–12 cm long (Iris). See 2.
1b—Fls small, petals 0.5–1.5 cm long. *Sisyrinchium bellum*.

2a—Fls yellow (can be tinted with blue). See 3.
2b—Fls blue. See 4.

3a—Corolla tube short and stout above ovary. *Iris hartwegii*.
3b—Corolla tube long and slender above ovary. *I. macrosiphon*.

4a—Western foothills. *I. macrosiphon*.
4b—East side of Sierra Nevada. *I. missouriensis*.

Genus *Sisyrinchium*

Sisyrinchium bellum—Blue-eyed Grass. Fig. 190. Plant low, 1.5 to 3 dm tall; fls with 6 blue-purple petals, flat,

[202]

bowl-like. Moist meadows, widespread. FW, MCF, MM. Feb–July.

Iris hartwegii—Hartweg's Iris. (See p. 155.) Fls golden yellow or paler, corolla tube above ovary short and stout, long (6–15 cm), slender pedicel below the ovary. Compare with *I. macrosiphon* to avoid misidentification. Dry shady woods on w. slope. FW, C, PP. March–July.

I. macrosiphon—Bowl-tubed Iris. Fls pale yellowish, or yellowish with blue tinting, or completely blue-purple, corolla tube above ovary long (5–15 cm) and slender with a small bowl-like enlargement at top, pedicel below ovary short. Compare with *I. hartwegii* to avoid misidentification. Dry shady woods on w. slope from Mariposa Co. north; most common species Placer Co. north. FW, C, PP. April–June.

I. missouriensis—Western Blue Flag. Pl. 16c. Plant in large clumps with stems to 5 dm. Fls blue. Moist or wet meadows on e. slope. MM. May–July.

"Big Medicine" to the Indians because of its many uses. Root tea was used for kidney trouble, and they claimed it was a positive cure for venereal disease. For toothache the root was inserted in the cavity to kill the nerve, which worked fine—except the tooth falls out!

KEY TO THE FAMILY ORCHIDACEAE (ORCHID)

1a—Lvs and stem green. See 2.
1b—Lvs and stem white to yellowish-red. See 9.

2a—1–15 fls per stem. See 3.
2b—More than 15 to several hundred fls per stem. See 5.

3a—Lower petal a slipperlike sac. See 4.
3b—Lower petal not saclike. *Epipactis gigantea.*

4a—2 large lvs, opposite each other. *Cyripedium fasciculatum.*

4b—Lvs 4–7 alternately up stem. *C. montanum.*

5a—Each fl with a definite spur. See 6.
5b—Each fl without a spur. See 7.

6a—Fls white. *Habenaria dilatata.*
6b—Fls green. *H. sparsiflora.*

7a—Plants of dry shady woods. *Goodyera obongifolia.*
7b—Plants of wet springy places. See 8.

8a—Fls greenish yellow. *Listera convallarioides.*
8b—Fls whitish in twisted spiral. *Spiranthes porrifolia.*

9a—Plant stem and fls yellowish to purplish. *Corallorhiza maculata.*
9b—Plant stem and fls white. *Eburophyton austinae.*

Genus *Cypripedium* (Lady Slipper)

Cypripedium fasciculatum—Clustered Lady's Slipper. Two lvs, large, ovate, opposite each other on low stem; fls 1–6, greenish-yellow with purplish veins, lower petal sac slipperlike. Deep humus soil in very shady woods, 3000–7000 on w. slope from Nevada Co. north. MCF. June.

Flowers shortly after snow melts. Plants of this species become quite old; I studied one that was at least 95 years old. Orchids do not transplant and picked flowers wilt at once, so leave them for others to see.

C. montanum—Mountain Lady's Slipper. Stems erect, 3–6 dm tall; 4–7 lvs large, ovate, alternately arranged; fls brownish-purple, slipper white with purple veins. Moist shady woods near streams below 6000 on w. slope, fairly frequent Yosemite and north. MCF. May–Aug.

[204]

Genus *Epipactis*

Epipactis gigantea—Giant Hellerborine or Stream Orchid. Pl. 16*d*. Stems stout, 3–9 dm tall; lvs ovate, 5–15 cm long; 3–15 fls, sepals greenish 12–18 mm long, petals purplish or reddish with the lower lip veined with red. On steep banks which have a steady flow of clean water all year, frequent below 7500. FW, C, MCF. May–Aug.

Genus *Habenaria*

Habenaria dilatata subsp. *leucostachys*—Sierra Rein Orchid, Crane Orchid. Pl. 16*f*. Stems single, erect ¼– 1 m tall; lvs lanceolate; fls many, white, with long spur, in a long spike. Semi-shady marshes below 11000, very common, often with *H. sparsiflora*. FW, MCF, S. June– Sept.

Recent research in the eastern United States has shown that mosquitoes are the pollinating agent for *Habenarias*. A careful examination of mosquitoes captured after a visit to our western species of *Habenaria* may well show the same results. Look for the pollina (pollen) sacs attached to the mosquitoes head or body.

H. sparsiflora—Sparsely-flowered Bog Orchid. Fls greenish, each with a long spur, in a sparsely flowered spike; stem 3–6 dm tall. Marshy places, 4000–11000, very common, often with *H. dilatata*. MCF, MM, S. June–Aug.

Genus *Goodyera*

Goodyera oblongifolia—Rattlesnake Orchid. Plant is low rosette of dark green lvs with white markings similar to the pattern of a rattlesnake; fls on a tall leafless stem, small, whitish. Dry semi-shaded woods below 8000. MCF. July–Aug.

The leaf pattern is so distinctive that this plant can be identified at any time of year.

Genus *Spiranthes*

Spiranthes porrifolia—Ladies Tresses. Pl. 16e. Stems 1–5 dm tall with a fl spike of tight spiraling white fls, much like a lady's long braided hair. Sunny marshes below 8000 on w. slope. MM. June–Aug.

Genus *Listera*

Listera convallarioides—Broad-lipped Twayblade. Stem low 1–2 dm tall; lvs very thin, oval, 3–5 cm long; fls yellow-green with broad lip. In very dense shady places close to the edge of flowing springs or streams, below 8000. MCF. June–Aug.

Genus *Corallorhiza*

Corallorhiza maculata—Spotted Coralroot. Stems in clumps, usually many, yellowish; fls also yellowish to purplish, lower fl lip white with purple dots. Dry shady woods below 9000 on w. slope. MCF. June–July.

C. striata—Striped Coralroot. Similar to *C. maculata*, but fls yellow with red stripes. Same distribution.

Indians thought the coral-like roots to be of supernatural origin. Dried plants were used in a tea for colds.

Genus *Eburophyton*

Eburophyton austinae—Phantom Orchid. Stems usually in clumps, 2–5 dm tall; stem and fls white, a saphro-phyte like the Coralroots. Deep humus in shaded woods below 7000 on w. slope. MCF. Late May–June.

USEFUL REFERENCES

Abrams, LeRoy. *Illustrated Flora of the Pacific States.* Stanford: Stanford University Press. Vol. 1, 1940; Vol. 2, 1944; Vol. 3, 1951; Vol. 4 with Roxana S. Ferris, 1960. S. Ferris, 1960.

Ewan, Joseph, ed. *A Short History of Botany in the United States.* New York; Hafner Publishing Co., 1969.

Harrington, H. D., *Edible Native Plants of the Rocky Mountains.* Albuquerque: University of New Mexico Press, 1967.

Heller, Christine A. *Wild, Edible and Poisonous Plants of Alaska.* Publ. No. 40. Cooperative Extension Service, University of Alaska. 1966.

Jepson, Willis L. *A Manual of the Flowering Plants of California.* Berkeley: Associated Students Store, 1923–1925. Reprinted, 1963, by the University of California Press.

Kirk, Donald. *Wild Edible Plants of the Western States.* Healdsburg: Naturegraph Publishers. 1970.

Martin, A. C., H. S. Zim, and A. Nelson, *American Wildlife and Plants A guide to Wildlife Food Habits.* New York: Dover Publications, 1961.

Medsger, Oliver Perry. *Edible Wild Plants.* New York: The Macmillan Co., 1939. Reprinted 1969.

Munz, Philip A. *A California Flora.* Berkeley: University of California Press, 1968, 1959.

Murphy, Edith Van Allen. *Indian Uses of Native Plants.* Fort Bragg, Ca.: Mendocino County Historical Society, 1959.

Public Service Office, Agricultural Extension Service, 229 University Hall, Univ. of Calif., Berkeley. Write for "The Selection and Preparation of Flowering Plant Specimens" and "An Annotated Reference List to the Native Plants, Weeds, and some of the Ornamental Plants of California."

ORGANIZATIONS

California Native Plant Society, 2490 Channing Way, Berkeley, California, 94704. Many local chapters in California.

The Nature Conservancy, 215 Market Street, San Francisco, California, 94105.

Sierra Club, 220 Bush St., San Francisco, California, 94104. Many local chapters in California.

INDEX

Achillea lanulosa, 174
Aconitum columbianum, 21
Actaea rubra, 21
Agastache urticifolia, 127
Agoseris aurantiaca, 187
  glauca, 187
  orange flowered, 187
  retrorsa, 187
  reverse pointed, 187
  short beaked, 187
Alfalfa, 146
Alismataceae Family, 192
Allium amplectens, 199
  campanulatum, 200
  obtusum, 200
  validum, 199
Allophyllum violaceum, 98
  Violet, 98
Allotropa virgata, 83
Alpine pynocoma, 176
Amaryllidaceae Family, 198
Amaryllis Family, 198
Amsinckia intermedia, 105
Anagallis arvensis, 79
Anemone drummondii, 22
  drummonds, 22
  occidentals, 22
Antennaria rosea, 188
Anthemis cotula, 175
Apocynaceae Family, 87
Apocynum
    androsaemifolium, 88
Aquilegia formosa, 23
  pubescens, 23
Arabis, 47
  divaricarpa, 50
  drummondii, 50
  glabra, 49

glaucovalvula, 49
  holboelli, 51
  lemmonii, 51
  lyallii, 50
  inyoensis, 50
  perennans, 51
  platysperma, 49
  rectissima, 51
  repanda, 49
Araliaceae Family, 155
Aralia californica, 155
Argemone munita, 41
Areneria kingii, 59
  obtusiloba, 59
Aristolochiaceae Family, 155
Arnica amplexicaulis, 184
  chamissonis, 184
  cordifolia, 184
  cordilleran, 184
  heart leaved, 184
  longifolia, 184
  meadow, 184
  mollis, 184
  nevadensis, 184
  seep spring, 184
  sierra, 184
  streambank, 184
Arrow head plant, 192
Artic pearlwort, 59
Asarum hartwegii, 155
Asclepiadaceae Family, 88
Asclepias californica, 88
  cordifolia, 89
  fascicularis, 89
  speciosa, 89
Aster alpigenus, 178
  adscendens, 178
  andersons, 178

brewers golden, 189
  entire leaved, 179
  integrifolius, 179
  long leaved, 178
  occidentalis, 179
  peirsonii, 178
  peirsons, 178
  western mountain, 179
Astragalus austinae, 149
  bolanderi, 150
  kentrophyta, 149
  lentiginosus, 150
  platytropis, 151
  purshii, 150
  whitneyi, 150
Avens large leaved, 136

Baby blue eyes, 102
Balsamorhiza deltoidea, 171
Balsamroot deltoid, 171
Baneberry red, 21
Barbarea orthoceras, 52
Bear grass, 196
Bearded tongue, 118
Bedstraw, 163
Bee plant, 117
Bellflower Family, 165
Bindweed field, 90
Birds foot trefoil, 147
Birthwort Family, 155
Biscuit root, 162
Bitter cress, brewers, 52
Bitterroot, 69
Black eyed susan, 173
Blazing star, 37
Bleeding heart, 42
Blue curls, mountain, 127
Blue dicks, 200
Blue eyed grass, 202
Bolandra californica, 132
  sierra, 132
Borage Family, 104
Boraginaceae Family, 104
Brassica campestris, 53
  geniculata, 53
  nigra, 53

Brides bonnet, 195
Brodiaea, 200, 202
  elegans, 202
  harvest, 202
Buckhorn, 81
Buckwheat Family, 70
  wild, 70
Bur Reed Family, 192
  pond, 192
Buttercup, california, 25
  creeping, 26
  eschscholtzs, 24
  prickle seeded, 26
  straight beaked, 24
  water, 24
  waterfall, 25
  western, 25
  western plantain, 24
Butterweed, arrowhead, 183
  california, 190
  common, 190
  clarks, 183
  dwarf mountain, 183
  sierra, 182
  single stemmed, 182
  wooly, 182

Calandrinia ciliata, 66
California spikenard, 155
Calochortus, 193
  albus, 193
  amoenus, 194
  leichtlinii, 195
  minimus, 194
  monophyllus, 194
  nudus, 194
  nuttallii, 195
  superbus, 195
Caltha howellii, 23
Calyptridium umbellatum, 68
Calystegia, 89
  fulcratus, 90
  malacophyllus, 89
  tomentellus, 89
Campion, bridges, 63

cuyamaca, 64
douglas, 64
lemmons, 63
menzies, 62
mountain, 64
naked, 62
sargents, 64
western, 64
Camus, death, 196
leichtlinns, 195
Camassia leichtlinii, 195
Campanula prenanthoides,
165
Campanulaceae Family, 165
Canchalagua, 86
Capsella bursa-pastoris, 55
Cardamine breweri, 52
Carrot Family, 156
Caryophyllaceae, 58
Castilleja, 123
applegatei, 124
breweri, 124
chromosa, 125
lemmonii, 124
miniata, 124
nana, 124
pruinosa, 124
Centaurea solstitalis, 168
Centaurium venustum, 86
Centaury beautiful, 86
Cerastium, alpine, 59
beerigianum, 59
common, 59
vulgatum, 59
Chaenactis alpigena, 189
douglasii, 189
hoary, 189
southern sierra, 189
Cheeseweed, 28
Chickweed, common, 61
Chicory, 188
Chimaphila menziesii, 83
umbellata, 83
Chinese Caps, 36
houses, 116
Chlorogalum pomeridianum,

196
Chrysopis breweri, 189
Cichorium intybus, 188
Cinquefoil, brewers, 137
drummonds, 137
slender, 137
sticky, 137
strigose, 136
Cirsium, 169
andersonii, 170
californicum, 169
drummondii, 169
vulgare, 170
Clarkia, 152
biloba, 153
elegant, 152
two lobed, 153
unguiculata, 152
williamsonii, 153
williamsons, 153
Claytonia lanceolata, 67
nevadensis, 67
Clemens mountain parsley,
162
Clintonia uniflora, 195
Clover, bowl, 144
brewers, 144
bur, 146
carpet, 144
clammy, 144
creek, 144
elk, 155
mustang, 94
small headed, 144
sweet, 145
white, 145
Cobra lily, 29
Collinsia, 115
heterophylla, 116
tinctoria, 116
torreyi, 116
torreys, 116
Collomia, 91
grandiflora, 92
grand flowered, 92
heterophylla, 92

linearis, 92
  narrow leaved, 92
  variable leafed, 92
Columbine, covilles, 23
  crimson, 23
Compositae Family, 166
Cone flower, california, 173
Conium maculatum, 159
Convolvulaceae Family, 89
Convolvulus arvensis, 90
Coralroot, spotted, 206
  striped, 206
Corallorhiza, maculata, 206
  striata, 206
Corn lily, 196
Cow bane, 159
  parsnip, 158
Coyote mint, 126
Crassulaceae Family, 128
Cream cups, 40
Creeping sage, 126
Cress, american winter, 52
  white water, 46
  yellow water, 46
Crowfoot Family, 19
Cruciferae Family, 43
Cryptantha, 104
  echinella, 105
  nubigena, 104
  pine, 105
  prickly, 105
  sierra, 104
  simulans, 105
Cucurbitaceae Family, 164
Cucumber Family, 164
Cushion stenotus, 177
Cymopterus cinerarius, 161
  grays, 161
Cynoglossum grande, 106
Cypripedium fasciculatum,
  204
  montanum, 204

Daisy, brewers, 179
  clokeys, 180
  cut leaved, 179

  dwarf, 180
  loose, 179
  nevada, 179
  short rayed, 179
  wandering, 179
Dandelion, alpine lake, 186
  common, 185
Darlingtonia californica, 29
Datura meteloides, 108
Delphinium, 19
  andersonii, 21
  glaucum, 21
  gracilentum, 20
  hanseni, 21
  nudicaule, 20
  nuttallianum, 20
  patens, 20
  polycladon, 21
  pratense, 20
Dentaria californica, 53
  pachystigma, 53
Desurainia, 54
  pinnata, 55
  richardsonii, 55
Desert trumpet, 73
Dicentra chrysantha, 42
  formosa, 42
  uniflora, 43
Dichelostemma pulchella,
  200
  volubilis, 200
Disporum hookeri, 197
Dock, 76
  curly leaved, 77
  few leaved, 77
  willow leaved, 77
Dodecatheon alpinum, 78
  hansenii, 79
  jeffreyi, 78
  redolens, 79
  subalpinum, 79
Dog fennel, 175
Dogbane Family, 87
Dove weed, 36
Draperia systyla, 100
Drosera rotundifolia, 29

Droseraceae Family, 29
Draba breweri, 57
  cross flowered, 58
  cruciata, 58
  dense leaved, 57
  densifolia, 57
  lemmonii, 57
  lemmons, 57
  paysonii, 58
  paysons, 58
  sierra, 58
  sierrae, 58
  stenoloba, 57
Dudleya cymosa, 129
  lax, 129
  spreading, 129

Eburophyton austinae, 206
Elephants head, 122
  little, 121
Epipactis gigantea, 205
Epilobium, 153
  angustifolium, 154
  obcordatum, 154
  paniculatum, 153
Eremocarpus setigerus, 36
Erigeron breweri, 179
  clokeyi, 180
  compositus, 179
  lonchophyllus, 179
  nevadincola, 179
  peregrinus, 179
  pygmaeus, 180
  vagus, 179
Eriogonum, 70
  frosty, 72
  incanum, 72
  inflatum, 73
  latens, 71
  lobbii, 71
  lobbs, 71
  marifolium, 72
  marum leaved, 72
  naked stemmed, 73
  nudum, 73
  ocher flowered, 74

ochrocephalum, 74
  onion flowered, 71
  ovalifolium, 74
  oval leafed, 74
  spergulinum, 72
  spurry, 72
  sulphur flowered, 71
  umbellatum, 71
  wrightii, 74
  wrights, 74
Eriophyllum lanatum, 180
Erodium botrys, 33
  cicutarium, 33
  moschatum, 34
Erysimum capitatum, 54
  perenne, 54
Erythronium
    multiscapoideum, 195
Eschscholzia californica, 41
Euphorbia albomarginata,
    36
  crenulata, 36
Euphorbiaceae Family, 36
Evening Primrose Family,
    151
Evening primrose, hookers,
    152
  low, 152
Evening snow, 94

Fairy lantern, 193
Felwort, 86
Fennel, dog, 175
  sweet, 157
Fiddleneck, 105
Figwort Family, 108
Filaree, long beaked, 33
  red stemmed, 33
  white stemmed, 34
Fireweed, 154
Five spot, 102
Flax Family, 35
Flax, small flowered, 35
  western blue, 35
Foeniculum vulgare, 157
Fragaria platypetala, 136

Frasera albicaulis, 87
    giant, 86
    inyo, 87
    kern, 87
    puberulenta, 87
    speciosa, 86
    tubulosa, 87
    white stemmed, 87
Fringe pod, 46
Fritillary, atropurpurea, 197
    purple, 197
Fumariaceae Family, 42
Fumitory Family, 42

Galium aparine, 163
Gayophytum nuttallii, 152
    nuttalls, 152
Gentian Family, 84
    alpine, 85
    hikers, 86
    sierra, 86
Gentiana amarella, 86
    newberryi, 85
Gentianaceae Family, 84
Gentianopsis holopetala, 86
    simplex, 86
Geraniaceae Family, 31
Geranium, family, 31
    california, 34
    californicum, 34
    carolina, 34
    carolinianum, 34
    cut leaved, 34
    dissectum, 34
    richardsonii, 34
Geum macrophyllum, 136
Giant helleborine, 205
Gilia, blue field, 97
    bridges, 97
    capillaris, 97
    capitata, 97
    leptalea, 97
    smooth leaved, 97
    tricolor, 97
Ginger, hartwegs, 155
Ginseng Family, 155

Globe lily, 193
Golden ear drops, 42
Goldenrod, western, 177
Goldfields, 181
Goodyera oblongifolia, 205
Grass of parnassus,
    california, 132
Grays lovage, 162
Grindelia camporum, 177
Gumplant, great valley, 177

Habenaria dilatata, 205
    sparsiflora, 205
Hackelia jessicae, 106
    sharsmithii, 107
Haplopappus acaulis, 176
    apargioides, 176
Harebell, california, 165
Hawkweed, shaggy, 187
    white flowered, 187
Helenium, 180
    bigelovii, 181
    hoopesii, 180
    tall mountain, 180
Helianthella california, 171
    californica, 171
Heracleum lanatum, 158
Hesperochiron, california, 99
    californicus, 99
    dwarf, 99
    pumilus, 99
Hesperolinon micranthum,
    35
Heuchera micrantha, 133
    pink, 133
    rubescens, 133
    small flowered, 133
Hieracium aliflorum, 187
    horridum, 187
Hollyhock Family, 28
Hookers fairy bell, 197
Horehound, 125
Horkelia, dusky, 138
    fusca, 138
    three toothed, 138
    tridentata, 138

Horse mint, nettle leaved,
127
Hounds tongue, grand, 106
Hulsea algida, 181
  alpine, 181
  pumice, 181
  vestita, 181
Hydrophyllaceae Family, 98
Hydrophyllum occidentale,
101
Hypericaceae Family, 39
Hypericum, 39
  anagalloides, 40
  perforatum, 40

Indian hemp, 88
Indian pink, california, 62
Indian rhubarb, 131
Indian warrior, 121
Ipomopsis aggregata, 97
Iridaceae Family, 202
Iris, Family, 202
  bowl tubed, 203
  hartwegii, 203
  hartwegs, 203
  macrosiphon, 203
  missouriensis, 203
Ithuriels spear, 201
Ivesia, 138
  club moss, 135
  dwarf, 139
  gordonii, 139
  gordons, 139
  lycopodioides, 139
  pygmaea, 139
  mouse tailed, 138
  muirii, 139
  muirs, 139
  santolinoides, 138
  shockleyi, 139
  shockleys, 139

Jacobs ladder, 90
Jewel Flower, mountain, 47
Jimson weed, 108

Knotweed, common, 76
  davis, 75
  douglas, 76
  leafy dwarf, 76
  kelloggs, 76
Klamath weed, 40

Labiatae Family, 125
Lace pod, 46
Ladies tresses, 206
Lady slipper, clustered, 204
  mountain, 204
Larkspur, 19
  andersons, 21
  glaucous, 21
  hansens, 21
  many branched, 21
Lasthenia chrysostoma, 181
Lathyrus, 146
  latifolius, 147
  nevadensis, 147
  sulphureus, 147
Leguminosae Family, 139
Lepidum deniflorum, 58
Lewisia, 68
  cantelowii, 69
  cantelows, 69
  columbia, 69
  congdonii, 69
  nevada, 69
  nevadensis, 69
  pygmaea   69
  pygmy, 69
  rediviva, 69
  sierra, 69
  sierrae, 69
  three leaved, 68
  triphylla, 68
Ligusticum grayi, 162
Liliaceae Family, 192
Lilium, 197
  humboldtii, 198
  kelleyanum, 198
  pardalinum, 198
  parvum, 198
  washingtonianum, 198

Lily, family, 192
  alpine, 198
  humboldt, 198
  kelleys, 198
  leopard, 198
  panther, 198
  sierra fawn, 195
  snake, 200
  twining, 200
  washington, 198
Limnanthaceae Family, 34
Limnanthes alba, 34
Linaceae Family, 35
Linanthus, 93
  bicolor, 94
  bicolored, 94
  bristly leaved, 94
  ciliatus, 94
  dichotomus, 94
  montanus, 95
  nuttallii, 94
  nuttalls, 94
  whisker brush, 94
Linum perenne, 35
Listera convallarioides, 206
Lithophragma glabrum, 131
Loasa Family, 36
Loasaceae Family, 36
Locoweed, alpine spring,
    149
  austins, 149
  bolanders, 150
  broad keeled, 151
  mottled, 150
  whitneys, 150
Lomatium nudicaule, 162
Lotus, 147
  argophyllus, 148
  broad, 148
  crassifolius, 148
  micranthus, 148
  narrow leaved, 148
  nevadensis, 148
  oblongifolius, 148
  sierra nevada, 148
  silver leaved, 148

  small flowered, 148
Lousewort, pine woods, 121
Lupine, andersons, 143
  benthams, 143
  brewers, 142
  broad leaved, 142
  covilles, 143
  farewell gap, 143
  dense flowered, 141
  douglas, 142
  grays, 143
  large leaved, 142
  lyalls, 142
  sickle keeled, 143
  stivers, 142
  tiny flowered, 142
Lupinus, 140
  albicaulis, 143
  andersonii, 143
  benthamii, 143
  breweri, 142
  covillei, 143
  densiflorus, 141
  grayi, 143
  hypolasius, 143
  latifolius, 142
  lepidus, 142
  micranthus, 142
  nanus, 142
  polyphyllus, 142
  stiversii, 142
Lungwort, 106

Madder Family, 163
Madia, common, 170
  elegans, 170
Malva parviflora, 28
Malvaceae Family, 28
Man root, taw, 164
Marah, horridus, 165
  watsonii, 164
Marsh marigold, 23
Marrubium vulgare, 125
Matricaria matricarioides,
    174
Mayweed, 175

Meadow Foam, Family, 34
  white, 34
Meadow larkspur, 20
Meadow rue, fendlers, 27
Medicago hispida, 146
  sativa, 146
Melilotus albus, 145
Mentzelia congesta, 37
  laevicaulis, 37
Mertensia ciliata, 106
Microseris nutans, 186
Milkmaids, california, 53
Milkweed, family, 88
  narrow leaf, 89
  purple, 89
  round hooded, 88
  showy, 89
Mimulus, 109
  angustatus, 114
  bicolor, 113
  bolanderi, 110
  breweri, 114
  cardinalis, 112
  guttatus, 111
  kelloggii, 114
  lewisii, 113
  mephiticus, 110
  moschatus, 111
  primuloides, 111
  suksdorfii, 113
  torreyi, 113
Miners lettuce, 66
Mint Family, 125
Mitrewort, brewers, 132
Monardella, mountain, 126
  odoratissima, 126
Monkey flower, bolanders,
  110
  brewers, 114
  common, 111
  great purple, 113
  kelloggs, 114
  lewis, 113
  musk, 111
  pansy, 114
  primrose, 111

  scarlet, 112
  skunky, 110
  suksdorfs, 113
  torreys, 113
  yellow and white, 113
Monkshood, columbia, 21
Montia chamissoi, 66
  perfoliata, 66
Morning glory, family, 89
  kern, 89
  sierra, 89
  sonora, 90
Mountain blue bells, 106
Mountain pride, 120
Mountain sorrel, 74
Mules ears, mountain, 171
  narrow leaved, 171
Mullein, common, 109
  moth, 109
Mustard, family, 43
  black, 53
  california, 52
  field, 35
  short podded, 53
  tansy, 55

Navarretia, breweri, 95
  brewers, 95
  divaricata, 96
  intertexa, 96
  mountain, 96
  needle leaved, 96
  sticky, 96
  viscidula, 96
Nemophila, 102
  heterophylla, 103
  maculata, 102
  menziesii, 102
  pretty, 103
  pulchella, 103
  sierra, 103
  spatulata, 103
  variable leaved, 103
Nettle, white hedge, 127
Nicotiana attenuata, 107
Nightshade Family, 107

Nodding scorzonella, 186
Nothocalais alpestris, 186
Nuphar polysepalum, 28
Nuttalls larkspur, 20
Nymphaeaceae Family, 28

Oenothera caespitosa, 152
  hookeri, 152
Olaski, 160
Old man in spring, 190
Onagraceae family, 151
Onion, narrow leaved, 199
  red sierra, 200
  sierra, 200
  swamp, 199
Orchid, family, 203
  broad lipped twayblade,
    206
  crane, 205
  lady tresses, 206
  phantom, 206
  rattlesnake, 205
  sierra rein, 205
  sparsely flowered bog,
    205
Orchidaceae family, 203
Oreonana clementis, 162
Orthocarpus copelandii, 122
  hispidus, 122
  lacerus, 122
  purpurascens, 122
Osmorhiza, 159
  chilensis, 160
  occidentalis, 159
Owls clover, cut leaved, 122
  copeland, 122
  hairy, 122
  purple, 122
Oxypolis occidentalis, 159
  western, 159
Oxyria digyna, 74
Oyster plant, 187

Paeonia brownii, 27
Paeoniaceae family, 27
Paint brush, alpine, 124

brewers, 124
desert, 125
dwarf, 124
gray, 124
great red, 124
lemmons, 124
wavy leaved, 124
Papaveraceae Family, 40
Parnassia palustris, 132
Pasque flower, 22
Pea, family, 139
  brewers, 147
  everlasting, 147
  sierra nevada, 147
  sulphur, 147
  sweet, 146
Pectiantia breweri, 132
Pedicularis, 120
  attolens, 121
  densiflora, 121
  groenlandica, 122
  semibarbata, 121
Peltiphyllum peltatum, 131
Penstemon, 118
  azure, 119
  azureus, 119
  bridges, 120
  bridgesii, 120
  davidsonii, 118
  davidsons, 118
  gay, 119
  heterodoxus, 119
  humilus, 119
  laetus, 119
  lowly, 119
  newberryi, 120
  newberrrys, 120
  procerus, 119
  rydbergs meadow, 119
  rydbergii, 119
  showy, 119
  sierra, 119
  small flowered, 119
  speciosus, 119
Peony, wild, 27
Pepper grass, 58

Perideridia bolanderi, 160
  parishii, 160
Periwinkle, 88
Phacelia bicolor, 101
  branching, 101
  caterpillar, 101
  changeable, 100
  cicutaria, 101
  common, 101
  distans, 101
  eisenii, 101
  eisens, 101
  hydrophylloides, 100
  mutabilis, 100
  quickii, 101
  quicks, 101
  racemosa, 101
  racemose, 101
  ramosissima, 101
  two colored, 101
  waterleaf, 100
Phlox, family, 90
  Phlox genus, 92
  covillei, 93
  covilles, 93
  diffusa, 93
  gracilis, 92
  slender, 92
  speciosa, 92
  spreading, 93
  stansburyi, 92
  stansburys, 92
  western showy, 92
Pholistoma membranaceum,
  103
Pine drops, 84
Pineapple weed, 174
Pink Family, 58
Pitcher Plant Family, 29
Plagiobothrys, harsh, 105
  hispidulus, 105
  nothofulvus, 105
Plantaginaceae Family, 80
Plantain, common, 80
  english, 81
  hookers california, 80

Plantago hookeriana, 80
  lanceolata, 81
  major, 80
Platystemon californicus, 40
Plectritis ciliosa, 164
  long spurred, 164
Podistera nevadensis, 161
  sierra, 161
Poison hemlock, 159
Polemoniaceae Family, 90
Polemonium, 90
  caeruleum, 91
  californicum, 91
  eximium, 91
  great, 91
  low, 91
  pulcherrimum, 91
  showy, 91
Polygonaceae Family, 70
Polygonum, 74
  aviculare, 76
  bistortoides, 75
  coccineum, 75
  davisiae, 75
  douglasii, 76
  kelloggii, 76
  minimum, 76
Pond Lily, yellow, 28
Popcorn flower, 105
Poppy, family, 40
  california, 41
  prickly, 41
  wind, 41
Potentilla, 136
  breweri, 137
  drummondii, 137
  glandulosa, 137
  gracilis, 137
  pseudosericea, 136
Portulacaceae family, 65
Pretty face, 201
Primrose family, 77
Primula suffrutescens, 79
Primulaceae family, 77
Princes pine, little, 83
  western, 83

Proliferous pink, 64
Prunella vulgaris, 127
Pterospora andromedea, 84
Pteryxia terebinthina, 162
   terebinth, 162
Pussy paws, 68
Pussytoes, 188
Pyrola californica, 82
   minor, 83
   picta, 83
   secunda, 83
Pyrolaceae family, 81

Queen Cup, 195

Radish, wild, 47
Raillardella argentea, 189
   green leaved, 189
   scaposa, 189
   silky, 189
Rangers button, 157
Ranunculus, 23
   alismaefolius, 24
   aquatilis, 24
   californicus, 25
   eschscholtzii, 24
   flammula, 26
   hystriculus, 25
   muricatus, 26
   occidentalis, 25
   orthorhynchus, 24
Ranunculaceae Family, 19
Raphanus sativus, 47
Rattlesnake weed, 36
Rattleweed, 149
Red larkspur, 20
Red maids, 66
Rhubarb, indian, 131
Rock cress, bent pod, 50
   blue podded, 49
   bristly leaved, 51
   broad seeded, 49
   drummonds, 50
   holboells, 51
   inyo, 50
   lemmons, 51

   lyalls, 50
   perennial, 51
   repand, 49
Rock star, 131
   fringe, 154
Rorippa, 45
   curvisiliqua, 46
   nasturtium-aquaticum, 46
Rosaceae family, 134
Rose family, 134
Rosy everlasting, 188
Rosy fairy lantern, 194
Rubiaceae Family, 163
Rudbeckia californica, 173
   hirta, 173
Rumex acetosella, 76
   crispus, 77
   paucifolius, 77
   salicifolius, 77

Saint Johns Wort Family, 39
Sagina saginoides, 59
Sagittaria cuneata, 192
Salsify, 187
Salvia sonomensis, 126
Sandwort, alpine, 59
   kings smooth, 59
Sarcodes sanguinea, 84
Sarraceniaceae Family, 29
Saxifragaceae family, 130
Saxifrage, family, 130
   alpine, 131
   aprica, 131
   bryophora, 131
   bud, 131
   california, 132
   californica, 132
   sierra, 132
   tolmiei, 131
Scarlet pimpernel, 79
Scarlet trumpet flower, 97
Scrophularia californica, 117
Scrophulariaceae Family,
   108
Scutellaria californica, 128
   tuberosa, 128

Sedum, 129
  lanceolatum, 130
  narrow petaled, 130
  obtusatum, 130
  rosea, 129
  rosy, 129
  sierra, 130
  spathula leaved, 130
  spathulifolium, 130
Sego lily, 195
Selfheal, 127
Senecio aronicoides, 182
  canus, 182
  clarkianus, 184
  integerrimus, 182
  fremontii, 183
  scorzonella, 182
  triangularis, 183
  vulgaris, 190
Sheep pod, purshs, 150
Sheep sorrel, 76
Shepherds purse, 55
Shooting star, alpine, 78
  hansens, 79
  jeffreys, 78
  mountaineer, 79
  sierra, 79
Sibbaldia procumbens, 135
Sidalcea, creeping, 29
  glaucescens, 29
  glaucous, 29
  harsh, 29
  malvaeflora, 29
  marsh, 29
  oregana, 29
  ranunculacea, 29
  reptans, 29
  spiked, 29
Sierra fawn lily, 195
Sierra pilot, 91
Sierra primrose, 79
Silene, 61
  aperta, 62
  bridgesii, 63
  californica, 62
  douglasii, 64

  lemmonii, 63
  menziesii, 62
  montana, 64
  occidentalis, 64
  sargentii, 64
  verecunda, 64
Silybum marianum, 169
Sisyrinchium bellum, 202
Skullcap, blue, 128
  california, 128
Sky pilot, 91
Sky trumpet, 97
Slender larkspur, 20
Smilacina stellata, 197
Snakeweed, 75
Sneezeweed, bigelows, 181
Snow plant, 84
Solanaceae, 107
Soap plant, 196
Solidago occidentalis, 177
Solomons seal, false, 197
Sonchus oleraceus, 185
Sow thistle, common, 185
Sparganiaceae Family, 192
Sparganium simplex, 192
Speedwell, 117
Sphenosciadium
  capitellatum, 157
Spiranthes porrifolia, 206
Spreading larkspur, 20
Springbeauty, lance leaved,
  67
  Sierra nevada, 67
Spurge Family, 36
Stachys albens, 127
Star flower, 79
Star thistle, yellow, 168
Star tulip, lesser, 194
  naked, 194
  yellow, 194
Starwort, chamissos, 61
  long stalked, 61
  sticky, 61
Steers head, 43
Stellaria, 60
  crispa, 61

jamesiana, 61
longipes, 61
media, 61
Stephanomeria lactucina, 188
large flowered, 188
Stonecrop family, 128
pygmy, 129
Storksbill, 33
Strawberry, broad petaled, 136
Stream orchid, 205
Streptanthus tortuosus, 47
Stickseed, jessicas, 106
sharsmiths, 107
Stylomecon heterophylla, 41
Sugar stick, 83
Sundew, family, 29
plant, 29
Sunflower, family, 166
common wooly, 180
Sweet cicely, mountain, 160
western, 159
Swertia, perennial, 86
perennis, 86

Tansy mustard, mountain, 55
sierra, 55
Taraxacum officinale, 185
Thalictrum fendleri, 27
Thelypodium lasiophyllum, 52
Thistle, andersons, 170
bigelow, 169
bull, 170
common sow, 185
dwarf, 169
milk, 169
yellow star, 168
Thysanocarpus curipes, 46
Tillaea erecta, 129
Tincture plant, 116
Tinkers penny, 40
Toad lily, 66
Tobacco, coyote, 107
Toothwort, stout beaked, 53

Tower mustard, 49
Tragopogon porrifolius, 187
Trichostemma oblongum, 127
Trientalis latifolia, 79
Trifolium breweri, 144
cyathiferum, 144
microcephalum, 144
monanthum, 144
obtusiflorum, 144
repens, 145
Triteleia analina, 201
hyacinthina, 201
laxa, 201
scabra, 201
white, 201
Tulip, leichlinns, 195
superb, 195
Tunica prolifera, 64
Turkey mullein, 36

Umbelliferae family, 156
Umbrella plant, 131

Valerian, family, 163
california, 164
Valeriana capitata, 164
Valerianaceae Family, 163
Ventana stick leaf, 37
Veratrum californicum, 196
Verbascum blattaria, 106
thapsus, 109
Veronica americana, 117
Vetch, american, 147
deer, 147
Vicia americana, 147
Vinca major, 88
Viola adunca, 39
bakeri, 38
glabella, 38
lobata, 37
macloskeyi, 39
purpurea, 39
sheltonii, 38
tomentosa, 38
Violaceae Family, 37

Violet, family, 37
  bakers, 38
  fan, 38
  macloskeys, 39
  mountain, 39
  pine, 37
  pioneer, 38
  smooth, 38
  stream, 38
  western dog, 39
  wooly, 38

Wallflower, douglas, 54
  sierra, 54
Wally basket, 201
Water lily family, 28
Water plantain family, 192
Water smartweed, 75
Waterleaf, family, 98
  california, 101
Western bistort, 75
Western blue flag, 203
Whitlow grass, alaska, 57
  brewers, 57
White fiesta flower, 103
White heads, 157
Whitneya dealbata, 181

Wild hyacinth, 200
Wild heliotrope, 101
Wild rhubarb, 76
Willow herb, panicled, 153
Winter cress, american, 52
Wintergreen, family, 81
  bog, 82
  common, 83
  one sided, 83
  white veined, 83
Wooly pod, purshs, 150
Wooly sunflower, common,
  180
Wyethia angustifolia, 171
  bolanderi, 172
  bolanders, 172
  covilles, 173
  invenusta, 173
  mollis, 171

Xerophyllum tenax, 196

Yampah, bolanders, 160
  parishs, 160
Yarrow, white, 174

Zigadenus venenosus, 196